# SPEAKING ILL OF THE DEAD:

## Jerks in New England History

# SPEAKING ILL OF THE DEAD:

## Jerks in New England History

## Matthew P. Mayo

Guilford, Connecticut

Text design: Sheryl P. Kober
Project editor: Lauren Szalkiewicz
Layout artist: Sue Murray

Library of Congress Cataloging-in-Publication Data

Mayo, Matthew  P.
  Speaking ill of the dead : jerks in New England history / Matthew  P.
Mayo.
     pages cm
  Includes bibliographical references and index.
  Summary: "The lives of notorious bad guys, perpetrators of mischief,
visionary-if  misunderstood-thinkers, and other colorful antiheroes,
jerks, and evil  doers from history all get their due in the short
essays featured in  these enlightening, informative, books. Speaking Ill
of the Dead: Jerks in New England History features  twenty short
biographies of nefarious characters, from  Charles W.  Morse, serial
monopolist, cheat, liar, and swindler, to Emeline Meaker  & Mary Rogers,
otherwise known as the Lady Killers"— Provided by publisher.
  ISBN 978-0-7627-7862-1 (pbk.)
  1.  New England—History—Anecdotes. 2.  New
England—Biography—Anecdotes. 3.  Outlaws—New
England—Biography—Anecdotes. 4.  Rogues and vagabonds—New
England—Biography—Anecdotes. 5.  Criminals—New
England—Biography—Anecdotes.  I. Title. II. Title: Jerks in New
England history.
  F4.6.M28 2013
  974—dc23

                                                              2013019011

Printed in the United States of America

10 9 8 7 6 5 4 3 2 1

*For Jennifer and Nessie, who remind me daily that life
is anything but jerky.*

*"All things truly wicked start from an innocence."*

—*Ernest Hemingway,* A Moveable Feast

Other Globe Pequot Press books by Matthew P. Mayo

*Cowboys, Mountain Men & Grizzly Bears:*
*Fifty of the Grittiest Moments in the History of the Wild West*

*Bootleggers, Lobstermen & Lumberjacks:*
*Fifty of the Grittiest Moments in the History of Hardscrabble*
*New England*

*Sourdoughs, Claim Jumpers & Dry Gulchers:*
*Fifty of the Grittiest Moments in the History of Frontier*
*Prospecting*

*Haunted Old West:*
*Phantom Cowboys, Spirit-Filled Saloons, Mystical Mine Camps &*
*Spectral Indians*

*Maine Icons:*
*Fifty Symbols of the Pine Tree State*
(with Jennifer Smith-Mayo)

*Vermont Icons:*
*Fifty Symbols of the Green Mountain State*
(with Jennifer Smith-Mayo)

*New Hampshire Icons:*
*Fifty Symbols of the Granite State*
(with Jennifer Smith-Mayo)

# Contents

# Acknowledgments

My sincere thanks to my editor, Erin Turner, for her help and kindness; to Belfast (Maine) Free Library; Doug Copeley, New Hampshire Historical Society; Nicole Cloutier, Portsmouth (New Hampshire) Public Library; Don Welch, Duxbury (Vermont) Historical Society; Schweitzer, Wikipedia; and Heather Moore, US Senate Historical Office.

My thanks, also, to New England and her hardworking people—stalwart, steadfast, and true (and who don't suffer jerks gladly); to my parents, Gayla and Bill Mayo, proud dairy farmers and native New Englanders; to my brother, Jeffrey, for having a great built-in jerk-meter (and to Jen, for putting up with him!); to my in-laws, Rose Mary and David Smith, for being so kind, so fun, and so strong; to my sis, Charity, fellow hermit!; to Gert and Larry Burdick, salt of the earth; to Nessie and Guy, for stepping out; and to the Royers and Pezzanis, who always know where Uncle Matt is.

I also thank all the jerks working daily to ensure people like me have stuff to write about for a long time to come. Keep it up!

Most of all, I thank my wife, Jennifer Smith-Mayo, for conducting all the historical image research and procurement for my books (and so much more!). And for her ceaseless patience, good humor, and warm smiles. You're a wonder. Hmm, how about some turkey jerky?

# Introduction

According to the *New Oxford American Dictionary,* a jerk is defined as "a contemptibly obnoxious person." But that, I have found, is a barely adequate starting point. True jerks deserve more robust epithets. How about scoundrel, villain, rogue, rascal, weasel, snake, snake in the grass, miscreant, good-for-nothing, reprobate, lowlife, creep, no-goodnik, scamp, scalawag, beast, rat, rat fink, louse, swine, dog, skunk, heel, slimeball, S.O.B., scumbag, scumbucket, scuzzball, scuzzbag, dirtbag, sleazeball, sleazebag, hound, cad, blackguard, knave, varlet, whoreson . . . okay, now we're cooking!

Call a jerk what we will, but at the end of the day, when history's details are scratched in the dirt, chipped in stone, scrawled on paper, or typed on a screen for all to read, "jerk" is still the best name for people who do bad things to others. Having said that, the term jerk is largely dependent on perspective. One man's jerk is another man's born leader, financial wizard, or ingenious inventor.

Let's face it: The world is filled to brimming with foul folk performing all manner of pernicious deeds and malicious undertakings. As one of the oldest settled regions in the United States, New England has had more than its share of insipid punks bent on performing nefarious deeds and naughty high jinks. And they're doing so in an effort to further their own ends and line their own pockets, usually at the expense of others—quite frequently those near and dear to them.

Given its age, New England's historic capacity for aberrant behavior is large, long, and legion. People whose clans proudly claim deep Yankee roots should also consider that if they look up into the gnarled limbs of the family tree, they'll see a number of jerks swinging from branch to branch, shrieking and gibbering and glowering for all eternity.

This book is packed with folks in New England who couldn't figure out how to stay on the straight and narrow, or more to the point, chose not to. No matter the excuses—war, insanity, psychosis, revenge, perceived self-defense, peer pressure, politics, or nature's wrath—jerk-like behavior is inexcusable, but frequently complex and always fascinating.

As with so much in life, the lives of these so-called jerks are rarely cut-and-dried. Some of them appear to have been born rotten (Seth Wyman, inveterate lifelong thief!), whereas others seemed to slowly don the mantle of scoundrel over time, and often through circumstance (Judge John Pickering, insane and drunk on the bench!).

While working on the book, it was important for me to keep in mind that much of the jerk-like behavior was, in the context of the times in which it took place, frequently seen as acceptable. But a jerk is a jerk, and I had no trouble calling someone on his or her offenses.

My reasoning was simple: People, especially adults, should have a sense of right and wrong, and the ability to differentiate between them. They should know, for instance, that pressing a man to death with stones isn't likely to get him to confess to witchcraft. Nor is it likely to result in anything other than a painful death and a messy job of cleaning up. Yet the puritanical brain trust running the Salem Witch Trials opted to crush poor Giles Corey to death. (He didn't crack, by the way. . . . Well, not mentally.)

Likewise, rational people should know that repeated and concerted efforts at diplomacy between a handful of leaders nearly always work better in the long run than a drawn-out, costly war in which hundreds of homes burn and thousands of people die. Yet Josiah Winslow and Metacomet couldn't quite find enough common ground to strike a deal for renewed peace, however rocky it might have been. The result of their pigheadedness? King Philip's War, the bloodiest, costliest war ever fought on New England soil.

In writing this book, I have come to learn that merely being well intentioned doesn't excuse one for being a jerk. Plenty of people believe they are doing good, but in fact they are acting as Beelzebub's right-hand helper. Just because they don't know the difference doesn't mean they aren't devilish.

Speaking of oblivious baddies, I exercised a bit of authorial license in making Mother Nature a jerk. But if anyone, either human or omnipotent entity, is deserving of being taken to task for causing widespread grief and strife throughout New England—more so, in fact, than any other jerk in the book—it is Mother Nature.

Some jerks are more obvious and therefore easier to label than others—murderers, for example. Within these pages are some of the worst of the worst in New England's history, vile killers who snuffed out the promising lives of kind, innocent people.

But there are others who, when viewed through the corrective lenses of time, reveal jerk-like qualities despite obvious positive contributions to society. In considering Lt. Bennett Young and Dr. Henry Perkins, we see that each in his own way believed in the ideals he was spearheading (furthering the Confederate cause and spreading the gospel of the eugenics movement, respectively). And yet their individual actions terrorized innocent people. It is also interesting to note that one grew into his jerkiness, and one grew out of it.

Likewise, a particularly jerky period or episode can be, if not forgiven, at least somewhat softened by later actions. Consider the aforementioned Lt. Bennett Young of the Confederate States Army. During the Civil War, he led a rebel raid on a sleepy little Vermont town close to the Canadian border. He and his chums robbed its banks and tried to burn the burg to the ground.

An act of war? Perhaps in his eyes, but from a Vermonter's perspective, a state that gave more than most to the cause, it was a vicious act of cowardice. And yet, in his later years, Bennett Young went on to become a revered attorney who advocated for the poor and for orphans and was, by all accounts, a noble man who did not drink, smoke, or swear (at least not in front of ladies).

With this book I worked to provide readers with an overview of several hundred years of New England history as represented by the region's reprehensibles. I also hoped to define and illuminate the fact that jerks are both born and made, and that even good people can become jerks. And if their episodes of nasty behavior are sufficiently heinous and horrifying, they should be outed.

As much as possible, the chapters are arranged chronologically by state. However, a number of the jerks profiled performed their misdeeds in more than one New England locale. An ideal case in point: pirates!

Those scurvy rats plied their pillaging trade all over New England waters (and beyond), but I placed them in the Rhode Island chapter for a number of reasons. Not least among these is the fact that at the height of piracy and privateering in Yankee waters, Little Rhody was a nexus of buccaneer activity. In fact, she benefited greatly in the form of kickbacks, bribes, hush money, and payoffs (some things never change!).

As a lifelong New Englander (barring a few forays elsewhere on the map), I found analyzing the history of these six states as represented by the foul, the bad, and the jerky to be a fascinating, somewhat voyeuristic, exercise. Writing it I felt as if I were rubbernecking at a highway car wreck. But history has a way of relegating woe and misery to a tolerable, if undiminished, distance as we glide along, oblivious to the fact that we will be that astonishing footnote one day ourselves. It seems, sadly, that there will never be a shortage of jerks. Nor a shortage of people who like to read about them.

I also found working on this book to be a humbling experience, one in which I said a few times to myself, "Yowza, how many times have I done that? Or that? Or . . . that? I hope I'm not remembered years from now as too much of a jerk."

Then I remind myself that though we may well admire the good people in life, it's the bad ones we remember the most.

—Matthew P. Mayo
Autumn 2012

## CHAPTER I

# Mother Nature:
## *The Biggest Jerk of All*

It might seem odd to the reader to paint Mother Nature with the jerk brush when the long pages of New England's history are filled with human jerks aplenty. But special exception must be made for this most powerful rapscallion who has caused—and continues to incite—no end of heartache and misery worldwide. The six demure colonies of New England, however, have received more than their share of that disheartening walloping, on the coast and far inland, for far longer than people have occupied this place.

But let's keep it manageable and consider some of the biggies that have occurred in roughly the time that people have been keeping records: Tropical cyclones, more commonly known as hurricanes, had slammed our land far earlier than when Europeans began taking note of such things as aberrant—and destructive—weather occurrences. Through the wonders of science, we know that hundreds, perhaps thousands, terrorized the New England region in pre-Columbian times, prior to European settlement here in the early seventeenth century.

### Hurricanes? Yep, we have those. . . .

In 1635, a category 4 to 5 storm that eventually earned the cumbersome but appropriate name of the Great Colonial Hurricane of 1635, unloaded its fury on Narragansett Bay on August 25, killing forty-six-plus people. A storm of that magnitude today would cause massive destruction and deaths due to the increased level of settlement, especially along the coast where millions work and play every day.

A half century later, in 1683—once again in late August—Connecticut felt the hammer blows of a mighty hurricane. A decade after that, in late October of 1693, flooding from another hurricane was so extensive that new coastal inlets formed and others disappeared. A dozen or more significant storms hit in the eighteenth century, and the nineteenth century saw twice that many of note.

Among them was the Storm of October 1804, an unusual blow that, though still technically a hurricane, dropped three feet of snow and killed nine people, leaving eastern Massachusetts the hardest hit region in New England. The next year, a hurricane pummeled Cuba, then traveled north and made its next landfall in the region that would become the state of Maine.

On September 23–24, 1815, what quickly became known as the Great September Gale of 1815 drove hard into New England, conjuring up an eleven-foot storm surge. Once again Rhode Island's much-savaged Narragansett Bay found itself the conduit as the storm rolled in, killing forty people. In addition, five hundred houses and thirty-five ships were destroyed, and the city of Providence experienced extensive flooding.

On October 3, 1841, an extratropical storm, the October Gale of 1841, sliced just eastward of the New England coast, but because of the lateness in the season, it brought with it copious amounts of snow and sleet, of which Connecticut received the brunt: Eighteen inches of the white stuff fell. Wind ripped apart houses and drove boats ashore, and New England fishermen caught at sea off Georges Bank were doomed: Eighty-one New England fishermen drowned. At the century's halfway mark, in early October 1849, a brutal storm made landfall in Massachusetts, killing 143 people.

The twentieth century was even more unkind to New England: Roughly thirty major hurricanes of note ruffled Yankee feathers. Of them, the southern New England coastal states—Rhode Island, Connecticut, and Massachusetts—were most often the hardest hit, particularly in August of 1904, in July of 1916, and again in August of 1924.

Less frequently, though with no less severity, storms made their way inland. In November 1927, a particularly violent storm loosed torrential rains and snow far into Vermont's Green Mountains, where the death toll hit eighty-four, as opposed to one death in Rhode Island.

A storm by which many others continue to be judged, the New England Hurricane of 1938, rolled up the coast in September as a category 3 storm, though in Connecticut, Rhode Island, and Massachusetts, winds reached category 5 in strength. The Blue Hill Observatory in Massachusetts recorded a gust of 186 mph just before the device expired in the line of duty.

Still considered the worst storm of its kind in modern history, the Hurricane of '38 killed seven hundred people, six hundred of them in New England—and most of those deaths occurred in little Rhode Island. It has become somewhat fashionable in recent years to label a particularly devastating blow as a "perfect storm," but the Hurricane of 1938 qualifies like few others. It is known by a number of names including the Great New England Hurricane, Yankee Clipper, the Great Hurricane, and most suitably the Hurricane of the Century—all are fitting.

The first major hurricane to strike New England full-on in nearly the seventy years since the previous big blow (the Saxby Gale from 1869), the 1938 hurricane began humbly early in the month of September 1938, off the Cape Verde Islands, off the west African coast. Within days it formed into a category 5 storm, and by the time it lurched up the East Coast of the United States and made its initial landfall at Long Island, New York, on September 21, it had settled in at a deadly category 3.

As with numerous previous storms, Rhode Island's Narragansett Bay proved especially hard hit by this hurricane. The bay's peculiar funnel shape allows storm surges to compound in intensity. In 1938, this unfortunate geographic attribute, coupled with unusually high tides due to a full moon, drove the already high waters sixteen feet higher than the high-tide level.

Given that the storm was a relatively recent occurrence, many New Englanders alive today recall the horrifying event with clarity. Many others had friends and family who were alive then. One well-remembered man, Walter Eberle, could easily have been forgiven if on September 21, 1938, he had decided to shirk his duty and not report for work as assistant lighthouse keeper of Whale Rock Lighthouse on Rhode Island's Narragansett Bay. But he was not the sort to do so, especially not with six kids and a wife. If only he had known what was coming, but no one did.

And more is the pity, for on that quiet, early fall afternoon, with sudden, hellish vengeance, Mother Nature ravaged the coast of Rhode Island. Eberle reported for work the night before, and in the morning, the seventy-three-foot-tall Whale Rock Lighthouse was gone—nowhere to be seen. The only thing left was a raw concrete nub where the structure had stood. Of Eberle's fate, there would be no sign until, in recent years, remains of the Whale Rock light were located at the bottom of the bay.

Just up the bay, a wave slammed broadside into a school bus carrying eight kids. The driver herded the kids out a window and onto the bus, and then another wave dragged them off. Only one boy and the driver survived.

It was a rare structure, be it lighthouse or beach house, that could withstand the constant, relentless pounding the storm delivered. Rhode Island's coastline was a much-changed thing following the storm. Entire beachside communities were washed away, and many coastal homes were dragged out to sea with their inhabitants still inside.

Each of the forty homes on the finger of land called Napatree Point, off Little Narragansett Bay, completely washed away. Following the storm, no sign of the little settlement remained. It was not rebuilt, and today it is a wildlife sanctuary. One home in Charlestown, Rhode Island, was picked up off its foundation and dropped onto the other side of the road, where it remained, inhabited, until it was torn down in the summer of 2011.

In Providence, a city in which much of the downtown is built on pilings, motorists were stranded, trapped in their cars during the mad rush to get out of the city—and then thirteen-foot flood tides barreled into the sea-level downtown, drowning many where they sat.

The storm, so powerful that its impact was recorded on seismographs in California, had been tracked and monitored for eleven days, and for much of the time it seemed to meteorologists that it would give New England nothing more than a glancing blow. But at the last minute, it shifted course and slammed into Long Island.

All told, seven hundred people died in the storm, six hundred of them in New England, with one hundred of them from the town of Westerly, Rhode Island. The storm system itself measured roughly five hundred miles in width, with an eye fifty miles across. Winds from the storm were clocked at the Blue Hill Observatory in Milton, Massachusetts, at 186 mph for one gust, while a sustained gust lasting five minutes held at 121 mph. Only one of several wind instruments remained standing to record what became the second-highest wind speeds ever recorded on earth. The Hurricane of '38 is remembered now as one of the three most devastating storms to hit New England since record keeping began.

A number of violent storms tracked through New England in the coming decades, among them Hurricane Carol in 1954, which left sixty dead. Hurricane Edna, just two weeks later, lashed Cape Cod and Martha's Vineyard, and then caromed out to sea before making landfall again in Maine, where it continued to cause severe damage.

In 1985, Hurricane Gloria, though a category 1 storm, nonetheless left widespread wind damage, among the worst since 1938, especially to New England's vast forests. In August 1991, Hurricane Bob whipped up tidal surges ten feet higher than normal, and wind gusts throughout the region topped 150 mph.

Now, at the beginning of the twenty-first century, New England has already experienced nearly two dozen tropical storms of varying degrees, some much worse than others. The most notable

*Half-submerged by storm swells from 1954's Hurricane Carol, Edgewood Yacht Club (Edgewood, Rhode Island) was one of thousands of architectural victims savaged by New England's notoriously harsh weather.*

COURTESY NATIONAL OCEANIC & ATMOSPHERIC ADMINISTRATION

thus far, especially given its rare utter devastation inland, was Hurricane Irene on August 28, 2011. Though it weakened into a tropical storm as it hit land, Irene still managed to pummel New England with brutally high wind and torrential rain that resulted in widespread flash flooding.

Vermont and New Hampshire suffered heavy property damage, and a number of historic structures, most notably covered bridges, were severely damaged or destroyed. Of the sixteen deaths caused by the storm throughout New England, ten of them were in Connecticut.

And then there's 2012's Hurricane Sandy, which was commonly referred to in the media as "Frankenstorm" because, as it drew closer to the northeastern coast of the United States, it combined with two other opposing pressure systems. The result was a massive system, one thousand miles wide and so slow moving that it took more than a week for its effects to vacate the premises. Though New England, particularly southern coastal New England, was lambasted by Sandy, the biggest, longest-lasting devastation was to coastal New Jersey and New York, with a death toll of 185 and damages estimated at more than $50 billion.

But wait! Those were merely the hurricanes. . . .

## It's a Nor'easter, by gum!

New England has long been the recipient of what the old farmers and old salts call a nor'easter. These nasty tempests occur when warm Gulf Stream waters heading northward collide with polar cold-air-mass winds traveling southward. Nor'easters are quite similar to hurricanes, though since they occur primarily in the autumn and winter months, they are more associated with heavy snowfall, flooding, and severe winds.

An ideal example of such a weather event is the Great White Hurricane, a four-day storm lasting March 11–14, 1888, during which fifty inches of snow fell over much of New England, most heavily in Connecticut and Massachusetts. The chilly crystals were backed with 50 mph winds from the northeast that stiffened into fifty-foot-high drifts.

Alternately known as the Great Blizzard of 1888, it has earned the distinction of being one of the most famous snowstorms in recorded US history, notably for its broad swath of destruction that ran from Chesapeake Bay up through New England and well into Canada's Maritimes.

One of the storm's claims to fame is the fact that it took place when New England was just waking up, stretching its arms wide and welcoming springtime after a particularly long and cold winter. Farm pastures were taking on a green hue, temperatures were rising into the low seventies, early flowers around farmhouse foundations were blooming, and leaves on trees were budding—a most welcome sign that spring was in the air throughout New England.

In Boston and other cities throughout the Northeast, people froze to death in their apartments for want of coal, while on the streets people who had ventured out into the storm for food or fuel were caught unawares and succumbed to bone-numbing temperatures. Bodies were found for weeks after the storm abated, seized in the rictus of death in alleys and doorways into which the unfortunates had crawled to get out of the biting wind and snow. Hundreds of people were stranded for days in above-ground trains in cities throughout the Northeast.

Though such occurrences were found to have happened most often in cities, the countryside, too, offered up its share of misfortune when the snows melted. Despite his wife's protests, one Massachusetts farmer went out into the maw of the raging storm to check on his stock in the barn, hundreds of feet away across the dooryard. His wife waited in vain for more than a day for his return, all the while the storm continued to hammer the house's shutters, clog the chimney, and peel shingles from the roof.

She prayed he had made it to the barn and had decided it would be more prudent to wait out the storm there, with the warm animals. But when the storm finally lessened enough in intensity for her to check, she found he was not in the barn. Where could he be?

It was another week before the massive, thirty-foot drift between the house and barn melted enough to slowly reveal the horrible truth. There were her husband's well-worn boots, then his legs. The rest of him slowly emerged as she pawed at the snow barehanded, crying and shouting against the inevitable. But his body was stiff and blue, and when she cleared the snow from his blue-black cheeks and forehead, his eyes were open wide, and his mouth, still packed with snow, was pulled wide in terror. He had never made it to the barn, but had frozen to death mere strides from the house. The farm animals were fine, if hungry.

Though coastal New Hampshire and Maine received lesser amounts of snow, the storm's damage there was nonetheless significant. The sudden drop in temperatures, at or near zero for days, combined with record snowfall driven at right angles by 80 mph winds meant visibility on land, and notably at sea, had dropped to near zero. Up and down the New England coastline, more than two hundred ships had grounded and wrecked in the storm's deadly grip. Half that number of sailors succumbed to the tempest-tossed sea. For months afterward, beachcombers found debris from wrecked schooners whose captains had had no option but to try to ride out the storm at sea.

Unfortunately for a number of them, they were unwittingly stuck in the shipping lanes, unable to navigate or know what direction they were headed. Ships collided with each other, and all hands were lost in terrible final moments with no warning but the too-late sounds of snapping timbers and cracking planking. The screams of the sailors were carried away on the hard, cold winds.

All told, four hundred people lost their lives in the Great Blizzard of 1888, half of them dying in New York City. Other cities mightily affected included Philadelphia, Boston, and Providence. Oddly, it was this storm that helped persuade officials in a number of affected cities that commuter trains and the dangerous sagging power lines, weighed down by ice and snow, should run underground. And in 1897, Boston became the first city in the United States to unveil an underground subway system.

The Portland Gale was another nor'easter that seemed to well up out of nowhere and hit coastal New England hard on November 26, 1898. Sinking 150 boats and killing 400 people, this vicious blow took its name for the side-wheel steamship the *Portland,* which fought to stay afloat and not turn broadside to the massive swells once its boilers went out. It collided with the schooner *Addie E. Snow,* and then both vessels sank. All 192 people aboard the *Portland* were lost, and only 36 bodies washed ashore. The wreck of the great steamship wasn't found until 2002, seven miles off the tip of Cape Cod; a quarter mile away lay the wreck of the *Addie E. Snow.*

Another particularly vicious nor'easter, the Halloween Storm of 1991, or what has been dubbed, in book and film, as the Perfect Storm, took place at the tail end of October of that year. Massachusetts received the heaviest damage from nature's vicious salvo, though its reach was felt from Puerto Rico all the way to Canada. Thirteen people died in the storm, one hundred homes in Massachusetts were destroyed, or nearly so, and further up the coast, off Nova Scotia, a one-hundred-foot wave was recorded. Six fishermen aboard the fishing boat *Andrea Gail,* out of Gloucester, Massachusetts, were lost at sea. Damage throughout New England and beyond totaled more than $200 million.

## Don't forget volcanoes!

And then there was 1816, the year that summer never came. Literally. Folks who lived through it called it "1800-and-froze-to-death" for good reason. And it all began with a volcanic eruption in the East Indies in April the year before. The volcano, Mount Tambora, erupted in tremendous fashion—the largest in recorded history— spewing ash and sulfuric acid high into the stratosphere. It was the largest such eruption in 1,300 years. Worldwide, the eruption and its aftermath killed more than seventy thousand people.

How could this so dramatically affect weather in New England—which was thousands of miles away—the following year? In short, wind currents. But it took some time.

In 1816, New England experienced killing frosts each month of the year. Crops such as corn, which were depended upon for human and farm animal consumption, never got a chance to grow to any significant height before being laid low by another frost. Cattle, poultry, sheep, and pigs starved in record numbers. People developed widespread diseases resulting from malnutrition, and many also starved to death.

Ninety percent of New England's much-relied-upon corn crop failed. Farmers were unable to pay their taxes and ended up losing their land and homes. The surviving members of many families simply walked away from their homesteads, unable to feed their stock or themselves.

New England would eventually recover from the detrimental effects of Mount Tambora's explosion, but for many it would be too late. Throughout the northern reaches of Vermont, New Hampshire, and what would become Maine, so many people left that entire towns were abandoned—many were never resettled. Some folks headed east to the ocean, settled on the coast, and turned to fishing to support themselves. Still others headed west in search of new, more fruitful regions to settle.

Given that so many natural episodes of savage intensity have affected New England in a relatively short span of time, it does beg the question: What's next?

## CHAPTER 2

# Gov. Josiah Winslow & Metacomet:
## *Warmongers*

Deep within the frozen heart of the Great Swamp, the Narragansetts hunkered within their huts while the bitter December day spit wind-driven snow and ice outside. Canonchet, their sachem, ruminated on the weather, on their current woes, and finally on their security. He secretly doubted their winter home would be sufficient should the fighting come to them.

Still, the winter home of the tribe was well chosen, sited as it was on a great, five-acre rise that benefited from being surrounded by thick alder growth. Beyond their palisade of upright logs, a forest of bare trees stretched away in all directions, though not thick enough to prevent the gathered warriors from keeping a sharp eye out for the English.

Metacomet, whom the English called "King Philip," was sachem of their friends, the Wampanoags. He had angered the whites many times over the years, and in many ways Canonchet didn't disagree with him—he, too, wanted the English to leave, to stop stealing land and killing his people. But this time, Metacomet had gone too far, and now the whites were calling the uprising King Philip's War.

War between his tribe and the white sachem, Gov. Josiah Winslow, echoed closer to the Great Swamp with each day. Winslow was a hard man to deal with—it seemed he wanted nothing less than death or slavery for all Indians. Did he not know that the Wampanoags, the Narragansett, and all the other tribes were here first, had been here since time began? Winslow was not like his father, Gov. Edward Winslow. He had at least seemed a kind man, willing to listen when Canonchet's people had something to say, and always he sought peace, for that was what they all wanted. But

*Josiah Winslow, 13th governor of Plymouth Colony, was not overly fond of Indians, but was, in fact, very fond of their lands.*

his son Josiah was filled with anger, and he was blind to kindness. Canonchet suspected that peace to him meant nothing at all.

So far, the Narragansett had been able to help the Wampanoag's women, children, and their old ones. But they'd heard recent rumblings that the English did not believe them and did not care that the Narragansetts wished to remain out of the fighting.

The Narragansett people had no love of the whites, but they had no love of fighting someone else's war, either—though if Metacomet's fight kept on as it had been, Canonchet saw no way to avoid joining him. Perhaps the Narragansett could hold out until springtime. And if he could, perhaps he might avoid having to send his own warriors to their deaths. The English, Canonchet knew, were fierce fighters and had more of the weapons he wished he had.

Canonchet sighed and closed his eyes. This was wishing for something that would not be. And doing so was a waste of time. He had to go outside, to feel the fresh wind on his face. Sitting much of the day in the warm hut had dulled his senses.

And at the same moment he parted the thick flaps of deerhide and felt the sting of the cold air, he also heard shouts. They arose from far off, by the wall of logs they had built to keep the English out should a surprise attack come. The shouts from his men, more of them now, grew louder. These were not men to raise their voices without reason.

Canonchet's heart beat faster, for he knew what this meant. He rushed toward them, already seeing through the gaps in the logs what he had long feared, but secretly knew was inevitable. The fight had come to them; finally it had come.

The next words he heard confirmed his fears.

"The English! The English have come!"

As if to leave no doubt, gunfire volleyed from the forest beyond the wall. Shots whistled, plunked into the logs, driving shredded wood and crusted snow into the chill air. Smoke plumed from the weapons of the advancing men, and now Canonchet saw more and more figures appear from the spitting gloom of the storm. The English made cautious but hasty progress as they stomped forward. Knowing they had been seen, they no longer made efforts to keep their presence hidden.

There were hundreds of English fighters emerging from the trees on all sides of the forest. His people would be surrounded, with little chance to get the children and women to safety.

Close by, one of his best warriors grunted and grabbed his stomach. He fell backward as if he were tired and needed to sit down for a minute. The man looked up at Canonchet with eyes wide in confusion. He tried to speak but blood dribbled out of his mouth. His hands dropped, and he fell to his side and was still.

The sounds of the fast-approaching horde and their weapons, combined with the shouts of his warriors and the screams and cries of the women and children just now beginning to realize the danger closing in on them, all rushed in on Canonchet in the time it took to exhale. Canonchet bolted back toward his wigwam, bellowing orders to his people.

His mouth was set in a grim, tight line as he ran to the huts, hurrying a small girl along toward her shouting mother. The Narragansetts don't want this; don't the English know that? Yes, he thought, some of our warriors had been helping Metacomet with his fight, but those warriors did not ask my permission. But even those rogue warriors were not to blame. The English were to blame. They had no right here, had never had any right to be here, and yet they took all they saw—and still it was never enough for them!

Ahead, Canonchet saw his people flee their winter homes, scrambling toward the forest beyond. They headed into the trees, deeper into the swamp, stumbling over the frozen, snowed land. They dragged children, and few of them wore clothing enough to protect them from the cold night that would follow such a foul day. Far to his left a wigwam smoked, and then blossomed into flame, the dry wood snapping and sending clouds of sparks skyward into the gray, heavy air.

Canonchet realized with the force of a gunshot what he had never really wished to believe before: The English want none of his people left alive; they want all the land. Never was there a people so unsatisfied. There would never be enough for them. They would only be happy when the Narragansetts were all dead. And yet he hoped he was wrong.

I will not let it happen, Canonchet vowed in silent rage as he bolted for his own weapons. Too late—he felt a sharp blow on his shoulder and turned to see a member of the English militia, no more than a boy, glaring at him with hate in his eyes. Why? Had Metacomet's warriors killed his family?

Canonchet heard a woman scream behind him as what seemed to be an endless number of English soldiers bore down on them through and around the uncompleted palisade walls. They had not finished building the protective wall before cold weather came, not believing they would really need it. And now it was too late.

The woman's scream stopped with a suddenness that meant one thing—and in that instant, Canonchet lost hold of any fine threads of hope for peace with the whites that he might have had. These English were here to kill them all: children, their mothers, grandmothers, and grandfathers. They were not here to take prisoners and humiliate the Narragansetts, selling them into slavery. Even that would be better than this. No, they were here to kill.

Even as he thought it, Canonchet howled his rage at the young white fool before him, then two, three others closed in. He shrugged off the thick layers of his wool blankets and slipped his long knife free of its sheath. And he lunged at the young soldier.

It is unfortunate that first-generation-American Josiah Winslow did not inherit more from his father—Puritan leader Edward Winslow, one of the original Pilgrims, and third governor of the colony of Plymouth—than an urge to lead his people. While that is certainly a worthy ambition, guided by personal biases, it can also prove a recipe for trouble. Sadly, Josiah led them into avoidable war. His father had for years successfully worked with the local native tribes in an effort to maintain a long-held peace between them and the English settlers of New England.

But when Winslow the younger came to power as military commander of Plymouth Colony in 1659, Josiah let his dislike of the Indians simmer uncovered on the stovetop of local politics. And the kitchen soon grew steamy.

Josiah Winslow's attitude coincided with the colonists' growing sense that, unlike their immediate forebears, they could do without assistance from the Indians. They felt no responsibility to seek or maintain peace with them. The younger generations of whites reasoned that since most of them were born in the New World, and thus firmly established in this land, they should amass what properties they could. They felt it was their birthright, after all. And if the Indians, whom most whites regarded as a decidedly lower order, were impediments to their success, then why not simply take what property they desired—any way they could?

This included Josiah Winslow, who in the years leading up to his assistant governorship in 1657, and then as thirteenth governor of Plymouth Colony in 1673 (and the first native-born governor), came to strongly resent the native Indians. All the while he became embroiled in efforts to "purchase"—which usually meant confiscate—large tracts of Indian-owned land. His reasoning was faulty at best, but since he was in the seat of power, there were few whites who disagreed with him and few Indians who agreed with him.

Josiah's accession was dreaded by many colonists and Indians, who saw his impending tenure as bringing an end to smooth relations between the two factions, something he'd been whittling down for years as assistant governor. It marked the beginning of a new age in which the English, having entrenched and established themselves in their new home, desired to be the dominant power in the region. And they went about it with increasing force, showing little tolerance of, or use for, the native Indians.

The English settlers regarded the Indians as an impediment to land ownership and to a growing urge for expansion. They also feared the Indians and longed for their removal, by any means available.

As this attitude simmered and bubbled among the English, by the 1650s a similar widespread resentment among the Indians toward the whites developed. The Indians were justifiably incensed that they were quickly becoming marginalized, forced off their native lands that they had inhabited for as far back as they could recall.

But the Indians were in part responsible for their own demise. They had been selling off their land—duped out of it in many instances—since the 1620s when the English first bobbed ashore and set up camp. Over the decades, a steady increase in the number of deeds to native land parcels transferred to colonists, many with the blessing of Metacomet, the Indian sachem known to the English as King Philip. He was, after all, reaping personal gain from these transactions, and this pleased him. But when the number of land sales increased drastically, even he became incensed.

Now that the younger Winslow was in the governor's seat, he was able to fully indulge his urge for land and power. He received a rude awakening in 1673, when he learned of the illegality of some of his real estate dealings in Plymouth. But as governor he helped push through legal alterations to the law that in turn allowed him to retain his wrongfully gained lands.

Unfortunately for the Wampanoag tribe, Metacomet was in many ways much like his counterpart, Governor Winslow. He, too, had an urge to amass a fortune, and he recognized that selling land to the whites was an ideal way to do so.

Metacomet had good reason to dislike Josiah Winslow, privileged son of an original *Mayflower* passenger. Unlike his father, who had gone out of his way for years to accommodate and nurture a mutually beneficial relationship between the Indians and the English, Josiah seemed to take an entirely different approach and went out of his way to exacerbate distrust between the groups.

Metacomet believed, not without just cause, that Josiah, then head of Plymouth Colony's military, had poisoned his brother Wamsutta, called Alexander by the English, who at the time of his death had been sachem. The truth of this story remains up in the air. Some historians say Winslow's guilt is probable given his enmity toward the Indians. Others claim it was mere coincidence that Alexander, an Indian for whom Josiah Winslow had no particular like, suddenly took ill while a reluctant "guest" at Winslow's lavish home. Prior to the forced visit, the sachem had seemed in perfect health.

Soon after his brother's unexpected death, Metacomet became the sachem and took on the name King Philip, bestowed on him by the English, a tongue-in-cheek dig at the fact that Metacomet believed himself the equal of no less than King Charles II and regarded everyone else as mere underlings.

By the summer of 1675, Metacomet/King Philip had many irate young warriors on his hands. He'd been assuring them for years that they would have the battle with the English they felt they needed in order to preserve what few parcels of native land remained. At the same time, he had had a long history of not resorting to violence and acquiescing to the English when cornered. But that was all about to change—the young warriors had had enough, and they demanded accountability.

The change they wanted would prove to be bad for both sides. Instead of extending a helping hand to King Philip, who by then was desperate to keep the peace among his grumbling tribesmen, Governor Winslow, himself ill with what was likely tuberculosis, continued to regard the Indians as nuisances and impediments to progress. He prosecuted one of King Philip's senior advisors for the murder of an Indian named John Sassamon, who the Indians claimed was a spy for the English.

This and numerous subsequent instances occurred that further proved that Governor Winslow was too obtuse, too egotistical, or too puffed with self-importance to consider offering assistance to King Philip. Had he done so, what was one of the bloodiest, most brutal, and costliest wars fought in North America, may well have been avoided. Diplomacy was always a possibility, but it was not something Winslow ever considered.

In August 1675 several hundred Indians surrendered to English authorities in Plymouth and Dartmouth, having been assured they would receive amnesty. At this point, Governor Winslow could still have worked at negotiation, as the fighting hadn't spread beyond localized skirmishes. Instead Winslow, along with the other members of his war council, overruled those promises of amnesty and had the surrendered Indians shipped off to Cadiz, where they were sold to the Spanish as slaves. For Winslow, this was a win-win situation: Money was raised to help fund the war effort. It also resulted in fewer Indians to deal with on the home front, leaving more native-controlled lands untenanted and less opposition to future land transactions.

During a fourteen-month period between 1674 and 1676, roughly one thousand native Indians were sold into slavery and shipped off during King Philip's War. These included Metacomet's wife and nine-year-old son.

In the midst of the feuding between Metacomet and Winslow, no Indians—and consequently no colonists—were safe.

What does all this have to do with little old Rhode Island? In November and December of 1675, one thousand militiamen, one-tenth of whom were Pequot and Mohegan warriors loyal to the English, marched against the still-neutral Narragansett, led by Josiah Winslow. Their mission soon became clear: Any Narragansett would be dealt with in the harshest terms.

On the fast-moving campaign, a number of abandoned Narragansett villages were found and burned. The colonists roved inland, leaving for dead the few Indians they came across. On December 19, 1675, Gov. Josiah Winslow led his men on the most brutal campaign of the war in a winter preemptive attack against the Narragansett people at their winter stronghold, a five-acre fort housing roughly one thousand Indians, in the midst of a massive swamp in what is now South Kingstown, Rhode Island.

The one-sided fight raged for hours, but in the end the heavily fortified location was breached by the militia. The Narragansett winter food stores were destroyed, their homes burned, and women, children, and the elderly were killed. All told, 300 Narragansett lost their lives. Though they had been taken by surprise, the Narragansett managed to inflict significant damage to the militia, injuring 150 whites and killing 70. Those Narragansett who did manage to escape fled deep into the swamp, but soon succumbed to their wounds or to the harsh winter elements, where it is believed hundreds more died.

The largely neutral Narragansett tribe, under the leadership of Canonchet, had tried to remain out of the rising tide of war. But since their lands surrounded much of Narragansett Bay and reached inland, and since their numbers were substantial, the Narragansett made the colonists uneasy. The English feared it was only a matter of time before the Narragansett sided with King Philip, providing him with yet more warriors and resources. It didn't matter to the colonists that thus far the Narragansett had remained out of the thick of the action and had merely offered shelter to women, children, and the elderly. The brutal resulting battle has since been called the Great Swamp Fight.

By April of the next year, the already gutted Narragansett tribe, driven to fight by the overzealous militia, suffered its final defeat when its sachem, Canonchet, was captured and executed. By August Metacomet was also killed—by a Native American named John Alderman. Metacomet's head was cut off and decorated the top of a pike at Fort Plymouth for two decades. His body was quartered and strung up in trees, and his right hand was given as a reward to Alderman.

The war ended soon thereafter, and though both sides suffered tremendous losses, the whites got what they were after—more land, more power, and less Indian influence in their lives. But it all came at a terrible price. Because Gov. Josiah Winslow and Chief Metacomet/King Philip for a number of reasons were unable to sort out their differences, as has been the case throughout history when hard heads come together with equally hard heads, innocent people suffered the harshest of consequences.

King Philip's War is still considered the bloodiest, costliest series of battles fought on New England soil, and it was the worst event to befall New England in the seventeenth century. It took just fourteen months for a dozen local towns to succumb completely to Indian flames, for high numbers of colonists to die, and for up to one-tenth of all white men of military age to die. There are no accurate records of the number of Indian lives lost.

# CHAPTER 3

# Pirates:
## *No Honor among Jerks*

In the late seventeenth and early eighteenth centuries in New England waters, piracy was rampant, and Rhode Island was most often the nexus of this roguish activity. Make no mistake, Maine, New Hampshire, Massachusetts, and Connecticut all saw more than their share of piratical activity. But it was the people of Little Rhody who managed to hang twenty-six of the scurvy-ridden rogues all at once! That incident remains the largest mass execution of pirates in the history of New England.

It is rumored (as it is elsewhere in and around New England's briny waters) that the coast of Little Rhody, which includes infamous Block Island, the history of which is riddled with pirates, is still home to a number of as-yet-undiscovered pirate treasures.

Consider the curious caves, one at Jamestown, the other at Newport, each alleged to harbor secrets stashed there long ago by jumpy freebooters. Who knows what loot their unexplored depths might yet reveal? Or Blackbeard's treasure on Smuttynose in the Isles of Shoals off Portsmouth and the coast of New Hampshire, where he is said to have buried a great stash of silver bars. And then there's the pirate's cave in the forest of Lynn, Massachusetts, where a rumored fortune in pirate haul still hasn't been unearthed.

Pirating in New England waters all began with a freebooter who went by the unlikely handle of Dixie Bull, known as New England's first pirate. Dixie was a London-born sea captain who ventured across the Atlantic in 1631 and found Boston to his liking as a home base. He first traded with the friendly Indians along the coast of what is now Maine. In 1632, while roving Penobscot Bay, Bull was attacked by French brigands. His merchandise was stolen, and Bull was not pleased. Reprovisioning in Boston, he

*A Buccaneer*

*The coastal waters of New England were plagued with all manner of swashbucklers in the seventeenth and eighteenth centuries—a number of whom are said to have buried treasure along the Yankee shoreline, still unrecovered today.*

LIBRARY OF CONGRESS

enlisted a crew of roughly two dozen men and turned to the dark side to help stave off creditors.

Despite the fact that it had been the French who had set him on this course, Dixie Bull instead attacked English vessels, as the English fleet offered greater opportunity for quicker wealth. Later that year, with an expanded three-ship fleet, in an audacious move Bull boldly rained a fusillade of cannon fire on the well-defended settlement of Pemaquid. Dixie and his pirates coursed ashore and ransacked the fur-rich trading town. This and other such episodes quickly earned Bull the nickname "the Dread Pirate," for his callous, brutal attacks on innocent settlers and traders.

His whereabouts some time following the Pemaquid attack become a bit fuzzy, historically speaking. Some say he was killed in a fight, and some say he joined the French, which seems unlikely, given that they were the ones to "force" him into becoming a pirate in the first place. Still another guess is that he returned to England to live a life of luxury.

There is also a long-standing rumor that he buried much loot on Damariscove and Cushing Islands in Casco Bay, Maine, and that it is still there, waiting to be found. No matter his fate or that of his loot, and despite the fact that he only plundered and pillaged between 1631 and 1632, Dixie "the Dread Pirate" Bull will forever be remembered as New England's first pirate, and he has been memorialized as such in a number of songs and stories.

In August 1658, along the Saugus River in Lynn, Massachusetts, pirates rowed ashore in the inky shadows and made requests for hatchets, shovels, and other such items at the local ironworks. They compensated the ironworkers with silver coins. This cozy arrangement worked for a while—until someone tipped off the local British garrison, and soldiers fanned out through the surrounding woods in search of the skulking pirates.

Soldiers soon captured three men camped in the woods nearby, but a fourth eluded them. That lone, lucky pirate, Thomas Veal, hid in a natural cave where it was rumored he and his fellows had stashed great treasure. As time went on, he took in work as a shoe mender and traded services for food and goods with the locals. It is not clear why a man sitting on supposed vast wealth would do so.

What is certain is that the poor pirate—if ever a pirate deserved pity, it is Thomas Veal—soon met his sad end in the Great Earthquake of 1658, when it rattled the region and dislodged a boulder, causing it to seal off the entrance to Veal's hideaway and the pirate—and his alleged horde of loot. The capped cave went undisturbed for two centuries before being breached by spiritualist Hiram Marble, who bought the surrounding five acres, convinced by the apparition of none other than Thomas Veal that the stories about buried pirate treasure were true. The Marble family spent decades tunneling and searching for Veal's treasure, but they emerged empty-handed. Today their efforts, known as Dungeon Rock, are part of Lynn Woods, a large municipal parkland open to the public.

And then there is the case of Samuel Cranston, native of Newport, Rhode Island, who as a newly married young man put to sea in an effort to raise capital. Alas, not long into his voyages, Cranston was captured by pirates. Missing for several years, he was thought dead by his family. Eventually, his wife agreed to marry again. But on the eve of the wedding, guess who showed up—yep, Cranston. Apparently everyone was most excited to see the wayward sailor. Even the annoyed groom-to-be bowed out gracefully.

Cranston went on to have a long, illustrious career as a politician, serving as governor of the colony of Rhode Island and Providence Plantations a whopping thirty times. Interestingly, Cranston's lengthy tenure as Rhode Island's governor fell smack-dab in the midst of the gravy years of North Atlantic piracy. It's no wonder, then, that Rhode Island's purses benefited greatly from kickbacks from a number of sea dogs who straddled the blurry line between piracy and privateering. At the time, privateering was a sort of legal and widely sanctioned form of piracy, much in use by the government during England's war with France, from 1690 to 1704.

Following the conflict, many privateers simply continued doing what they'd been legally charged with doing during the war, but now they were considered pirates. Even the Piracy Act 1698, which outlawed all piracy, did little to stem the flow of this lucrative trade.

Not without ample evidence was Cranston accused of playing footsy with pirates, and he subsequently took the brunt of anger from England's bulldog, Lord Bellomont, who was known as the "enemy of New England." His criticisms referred to Rhode Island's government as "the most irregular and illegal in their administration that ever any English government was."

In a letter to England's Board of Trade, Bellomont accused Governor Cranston of "conniving at pirates, and making Rhode Island their sanctuary." In truth, Bellomont, a pompous, self-righteous windbag, wasn't wrong. Rhode Island profited mightily from the gray-shaded, less-than-savory pursuits of numerous privateers/pirates.

Capt. William Kidd was one of the most famous privateers of his day, having received his original commission in 1695 by the aforementioned Lord Bellomont, who was at the time governing a vast region including New York, Massachusetts, and New Hampshire, and was hard-pressed to rid his waters of pirates. Kidd's official letters of marque, signed by England's King William III, granted him official status as a privateer.

Among numerous locations worldwide that are claimed to be spots at which Kidd hid treasure, Rhode Island's Block Island is one of the more probable. In 1699, Kidd visited Block Island and was treated well by one Mercy Raymond. For her kindnesses, Kidd is said to have filled her outstretched apron with coins and jewels. He was eventually tricked into clemency and transported back to England in chains, wrongfully accused of being a pirate and a murderer. He was executed and his body gibbeted at the mouth of the Thames for three years.

Many years later, near Fall River, Massachusetts, an old woman who lived alone was dragged from her hut by locals who suspected her of witchcraft. They killed her, and in looting her hut later, they found an old, faded love letter from Captain Kidd, revealing that she was his long-ago lover.

The Ocean State claims another infamous buccaneer, Thomas Tew, known as "the "Rhode Island Pirate," though only because he lived in Newport at one time. No one is quite sure if he was born in England or New England. But he did his pirating/privateering far from New England waters. He also only engaged in two pirate runs, albeit significant runs, on which he made a ton of money for himself and the owners of his ship, the *Amity*. While he lived the high life for a time, enjoying the company of his good friend, New York governor Benjamin Fletcher, Tew's second big pirate cruise did not end as well. In September 1695, Thomas Tew was disemboweled by a cannon shot while attacking another ship on the Red Sea.

Little more than twenty years later, off the tip of Cape Cod on April 27, 1717, Black Sam Bellamy, a notorious pirate captain in New England waters, neared his home port of Cape Cod aboard his recently captured ship, the *Whydah*. He and his crew were caught in a vicious tempest that stripped the rigging bare. The boat foundered in forty-foot waves and 70 mph gusts.

As horrific as those final moments must have been for the pirates, Bellamy and his crew brought it on themselves. There's no way of knowing if a boat less weighed down by pillaged goods might have made it through the storm, but it was a near certainty that the *Whydah* would not, already riding low, stuffed as it was to the gunwales with stolen loot—between four and five tons of gold, silver, jewels, and more, plus sixty cannons that shifted in the hold as the ship rolled and heaved side to the waves. The ship split apart, and its wreckage was strewn for four miles along the bottom of the ocean. Two of the 144-man crew survived the wreck, and 102 bodies washed ashore.

Seven miles south on that same fateful night, the storm claimed another of Bellamy's ships, from which only seven men survived. Of the nine men who lived through both wrecks, six were tried and hung in Boston for piracy, though weeks earlier King Charles had signed an order pardoning pirates. Alas, the news arrived too late for the *Whydah* crew.

Bellamy's lover, Maria "Goody" Hallett, watched from the shore as her beloved captain's ship went down. Locals eventually tired of her roaming and moaning, so being practical and tidy New Englanders, they condemned her for being a witch and killed her. Undaunted, her ghost is said to still walk Wellfleet's coast today, pining for her pirate love.

In 1984, explorer Barry Clifford discovered the wreck and founded the *Whydah* Pirate Museum in Provincetown, Massachusetts. To date he has recovered nearly 250 million artifacts from the wreck.

Another overly romanticized pirate who is said to have had a rare affinity for the seacoast of New England was William Teach, aka Blackbeard. His was a three-year career, ranging from 1716 through 1718, during which he plundered a number of ships. Teach was married six times, and he kept a young woman as a mistress—or they may have been married—on the island of Smuttynose, one of the Isles of Shoals off the coast of Maine and New Hampshire, the very locale at which it is said he buried a fortune in silver bars.

Teach made his mistress/wife promise she would tell no one the whereabouts of the ill-gotten goods. And she never did—even after he was killed in a bloody battle off Ocracoke Island, North Carolina, suffering numerous pistol, musket, knife, and cutlass wounds that smoked and sliced their way through his tattered garb.

What makes a pirate a jerk? Pop cultural references aside, there are few instances of pirates behaving magnanimously. In truth, they were thugs afloat, thieving cargo, ships, and people from individuals or entities who had, for the most part, worked hard and operated (largely) legally to fund their vessels. A common pirate found roaming the New England coast in the seventeenth century was no better than a modern lowlife bandit who today strolls into a bank wearing a ski mask and brandishing a gun.

A good many of those old-time romanticized pirates went a few steps beyond merely robbing ships, however. Not content with the plunder, they frequently also tortured their captives, set them adrift without food or water, killed them outright, crippled or burned what ships they didn't want for their own growing fleets, and left a bloody slick of death and destruction on the waters of the North Atlantic.

The most despicable of these—and undisputed High Jerk of All Pirates—has to be Capt. Edward "Ned" Low. And his relationship with New England, and Rhode Island in particular, is a curious one.

Captain Ned plundered, looted, pillaged, and murdered his way up and down the Atlantic Coast of the United States from the years 1721 to 1724. But in July 1723, his flagship, *Ranger,* and twenty-six of his men were captured by the HMS *Greyhound,* which was sent on a mission specifically to capture Low and his band of foul freebooters. On July 19, 1723, the men were hung en masse on Long Wharf in Newport, and then buried between the high- and low-tide lines off Goat Island. And ol' Captain Ned was nowhere to be found. He had absconded with a ship, a much-reduced crew, and his life. But Ned was inconsolable, and his rage was beyond reason, not for the loss of his friends' lives, mind you, but because the unexpected turn in his fortunes cost him time and money. What can we expect from a man who, by all accounts, was the foulest, most murderous pirate to ever sail the sea?

Captain Low still had a ship and a crew, so he went back to work. First, he attacked a whaling ship out of Boston, sliced off the captain's ears, and forced the man to eat them before killing him. Then he looted the ship of everything not nailed down, crippled the mast, and set the crew adrift to starve.

Next he turned his sights on a trio of fishing vessels off the coast of Rhode Island, managed to decapitate the captain of one, burned that boat, and then set the other boats drift. Not surprisingly, the seething scavenger's rage was still not appeased. He captured two more boats, and his yen for torture became so disgusting and lurid that even his normally foul crew could no longer stomach the man's deviant ways. They refused his orders to participate in any further sadistic treatment he had planned for the unfortunate captives.

Low's preferred summer playground was the North Atlantic waters from the Isles of Shoals to Nova Scotia. It is said he looted and burned one hundred ships in his relatively short-lived three-year career. But when the man was active, he was most definitely active.

In the month of June 1722 alone, Low overtook and captured thirteen fishing vessels from New England. He was not without his own code, however warped it might have been. He usually offered the captured sailors an ultimatum—join him or die. Not surprisingly, most of the hapless fishermen chose to live as pirates rather than die at the hands of a torturing madman. Nasty Ned kept the largest ship of this fleet of thirteen as his new flagship, and then burned the rest.

If ever there was an anti-jerk in the story of vicious Ned Low, it is Philip Ashton of Marblehead, Massachusetts. He was one of the New England fishermen pressed into Low's service that day, but unlike the others, he refused to accept and sign the ship's articles, which would stamp him as agreeing to a life of piracy. This was regarded as a binding agreement for which he could be tried (and found guilty) in a court of law, should he survive to reach such a place. Oddly enough, the obstinate Ashton was not killed, but clubbed and whipped repeatedly, then chained in the belly of the ship, where he lived under a constant threat of death.

Remarkably, Ashton escaped, only to live life as a castaway for sixteen months on the small, uninhabited island of Roatán in the Bay of Honduras. He was eventually picked up by a ship from his home state of Massachusetts and wrote a long account of his fascinating ordeal. Alas, it was considered too outlandish, and the general public regarded it as a fiction.

Low's tortures, meanwhile, continued unabated—if anything they increased in frequency and sadism. He is reported to have sliced off the lips of a Portuguese captain who had cheated Low out of gold by dropping it overboard instead of handing it over. He broiled the man's lips, and then forced the man to eat his own lips before murdering the crew.

Low also captured a Spanish galleon, the *Montcova,* and then personally slaughtered fifty-three of its crew, forcing one of the crew to eat the heart of another before killing the man. He also burned a French cook alive because, as Low said, the man was "greasy and would fry well."

How did Captain Ned meet his own end? Somewhat fittingly, it would seem. Though several versions of his final days are popularly tossed about, the one that most people settle on as close to the truth has him set adrift, provisionless, in a small, open boat by his own crew, who had become increasingly weary of the deranged sea tyrant's tiresome and unpredictable humors.

As luck would have it—his sort of luck, anyway—Low only drifted for two days before being picked up by a French ship. His good fortune didn't last long, however, as his identity was discovered. The French whipped up a quick trial, and then hung him in 1724 in Martinique, before drawing and quartering his vile hide.

All these reasons and, sadly, numerous others easily qualify Low as the supreme piratical jerk of any and all seas during the golden age of piracy. He is but one of dozens of recognized pirates and privateers turned swashbucklers who continued to ply their illegal and immoral trade for far too long. Modern folk tend to color the past with rosy hues showing pirates in an undeserving heroic light. But truth be told, they were mere thugs of the sea, thieves who plied shameful deeds in uncommon ways.

Not all of New England's pirates were men, however. While the trade was definitely not an equal-opportunity employer, a foul cur named Rachel Wall, housemaid turned pirate, was perhaps one of the jerkiest of them all. As a girl on a small, rocky Pennsylvania farm, young Rachel dreamed of running away with a big, handsome stranger. And that's just what she did. She met George Wall, a sailor with larceny in mind. And it wasn't long before her beau and his roguish cohorts set up a devilishly clever plan to bring their victims to them.

They crippled their ship just enough to make it appear as if it were adrift, with none aboard but a hapless woman, teasingly half clad, weeping and howling for help, clinging to the rigging for dear life. When vessels drew alongside to lend assistance, Rachel's paramour and his gang of brigands would board the obliging craft, slay the crew, loot the ship's wares, and then scuttle the ship.

This they did most effectively for a time, especially in the busy waters off the Isles of Shoals, until they were caught at their own game. During a storm, George and his crew were washed overboard and Rachel had to perform her act for real. Luckily for her a nearby ship caught sight of her frantic gestures and heard her shouted pleas.

Back on land, she tried to find work as a housemaid once again, but ended up turning to prostitution with sailors at the docks in Boston, many of whom she stole from, and one of whom she murdered. Her undoing came when she attacked a young woman in the street one day because she fancied the girl's pretty bonnet. When the girl screamed for help, Rachel tried to silence her by ripping out the girl's tongue. Wall was hauled to court, where she was found guilty of the theft of numerous items and of the murder of a sailor.

In court she howled at the judge that she was not a murderer but a pirate, and she demanded to be treated as one. The judge had her silenced and read her sentence: For the murder, she would be hung to death on October 8, 1789. The judge closed his pronouncement with these words: "May God in his infinite wisdom have mercy on your black soul. For no one else will!"

Incidentally, she was the first American-born woman to become a pirate, and the last woman hung in Massachusetts. But she was not hung for piracy, as was her wish—merely for murder. Ah, the disappointment of it all.

## CHAPTER 4

# The Troubled Tuttles:
# *Flirts, Adulterers, Murderers!*

J ust because you're crazy doesn't mean you're not a jerk. Just because you're a jerk mostly to your own family doesn't excuse you from being regarded as a jerk by others. Case in point: those terribly twisted and cantankerous Tuttles.

Though the world had seen its share of odd behavior well before the fateful union of William and Elizabeth Tuttle, it is this Connecticut couple's offspring who took crazy to all-new heights.

Of their twelve children, David, Elizabeth, and Mercy were found by seventeenth-century courts to be decidedly *not* of their right minds, or as the courts put it, *non compos mentis*—"not having control of one's mind." Even some of the other Tuttle children not deemed legally insane gave lawmakers pause for reconsideration.

In 1660, at approximately age eighteen, Sarah, the seventh child of the dozen, was caught at a social function exchanging more than pleasantries with a Dutch sailor by the name of Jacob Murline. The pair was accused of "sitting down on a chest together, his arm about her waist and her arm upon his shoulder or about his neck, and continuing in this sinful position about half an hour, in which time he kissed her and she kissed him, and they kissed one another."

All this serious sinning had been witnessed by several viewers . . . for half an hour. In the context of our freewheeling, loose-as-an-escaped-con modern times, the above dalliance might seem like little more than a harmless game of slap and tickle. But in seventeenth-century New England, it was considered bold play for both the girl and the boy, and the societal level of tolerance for such behavior was nil.

Soon after the episode, this extended sin break was reported to Sarah Tuttle's father. Suitably incensed, he took the matter to court before none other than Gov. John Winthrop Jr. in hopes of rescuing his wayward lamb's sullied reputation. Judging from the young woman's experienced antics, daddy's efforts came too little, too late.

Given the laws of the time, and the fact that he had a dozen mouths to feed, Papa Tuttle was probably more concerned with recovering the damages that his sinful little sexpot of a daughter had so earnestly earned for him. A law of the time stated that "whosoever should inveigle or draw away the affections of any maid or maid servant for himself or others, without first obtaining the consent of parents or guardians, should pay besides all the damages the parent might sustain, 40 shillings for the first offense, and for the second toward the same person, 4 pounds and for the third, fined, imprisoned and corporally punished, as the Plantation court may direct."

Governor Winthrop labeled Sarah Tuttle as a "bold virgin," and the girl was no doubt snickering into her hanky even as she agreed that she was a sorry thing and that being sinful was something with which "she hoped God would help her to carry it better for time to come." He warned her to change her ways, or else. Witnesses reported that the threat prompted the coquette to nod emphatically.

Then the governor turned his righteous gaze on the Dutch paramour, Murline, whose carriage Winthrop said "hath beene very evil and sinfull" and that it "doth greatly aggravate." Winthrop also told the young man, apparently after having witnessed Sarah's powers of persuasion firsthand, that he should "shun such virgins as Sarah."

As a parting shot, and because punishment in such an instance in which the suspects apparently received mutual beneficence, Governor Winthrop took the democratic route, split the normal fine of forty shillings, and made them each pay twenty.

Such scandalous behavior would come back to haunt Sarah some sixteen years later when Sarah was struck dead in a manner most Tuttlelike. By then, Sarah was named Sarah Slauson, wife of John Slauson, with whom she had settled into a happy, matronly life.

On the evening of November 17, 1676, John had gone off on civic business for the evening. Sarah sat in her customary place by the fireside, with her children in attendance. Her twenty-nine-year-old brother Benjamin was also there visiting, and it is supposed that since their father, William Tuttle, had died a few short years before, in June 1673, that they might well be arguing over the division of his assets. Being siblings, they no doubt knew how to test each other's patience. The air in the room that night was tinged with the bitter rancor of argument.

Sarah mentioned out loud that she was sorry her husband hadn't eaten his supper before heading out for his evening's work. Benjamin said curtly that the man should well have eaten before he left. Sarah replied, "You need not be so short."

This was apparently enough to set off Benjamin's inherited hair-trigger temper. He rose from his seat and left the room in haste. One of Sarah's children, a daughter named Sarah as it happens, rose to shut the door behind her uncle just as the man returned. He'd been to the barn, retrieved an axe, and strode back into the room. He immediately struck his sister on the head from behind. "I will teach you to scold!" he growled, then drove the axe into her repeatedly, in front of her horrified children.

The first blow dropped Sarah the elder to the stone hearth. She never uttered a sound nor rose again as her children howled in horror. This seemed to snap the murderer from his frenzy of bloodlust—he dropped the weapon and bolted from the house into the night. Benjamin Tuttle hid himself in nearby woods but was soon apprehended. The once-flirtatious Sarah had reached the extreme end of her days and was likely dead soon after the first blow.

Two of the Slauson children, John and Sarah, aged twelve and nine respectively, gave evidence to the above event before the court, where it was judged that the head wounds Sarah Slauson suffered at the hands of her brother, Benjamin Tuttle, were the sole cause of her death.

"A verdict of a Jury's Inquest in Stamford, November 18th, 1767 on the death of Sarah Slauson, wife to John Slauson; who was found barbarously slain in her own house, as follows: We whose names are here under written (of the Jury) and how agreed under oath declare: the body of the woman we found lying dead across the hearth, with her head in the corner of the chimney wounded after this manner: the skull and jaw extremely broken, from the jaw to her neck, and so to the crown of the head, on the right side of the same, with part of her brains out, which ran out at a hole, which was struck through her head, behind the ear. Judging the weapon with which it was done to be with a narrow ax that lay near her, which was much bloody about the pool of the same, and upon inquisition from the children of John and Sarah Slauson."

On May 29, 1677, Benjamin Tuttle was tried in a court of law and convicted of the murder of his sister, "there to be hanged by the neck till he dyes & then out downe & buryed." And that is exactly what happened to Benjamin Tuttle on June 13, 1677, at New Haven, Connecticut.

But wait . . . you thought that might be enough tragedy for one family? Not hardly—get a load of Mercy Tuttle, sister of Sarah and Benjamin. It seems that in addition to insanity, the axe was the Tuttle family weapon of choice. Mercy, something of which she held in name only, was born on April 27, 1650, the eleventh child of William and Elizabeth. Early records indicate that when she was fourteen, someone accused her of stealing liquor (and then drinking it!). Ah, those wily Tuttle girls. Following this, Mercy seemed to have kept herself out of the record books, if not necessarily out of trouble, for the next quarter century.

In 1667 she married Samuel Brown and begat six children. And apparently life was good for seventeen years. Then one day Mercy informed her husband that she would have the children buried in the barn. When he told her the children were well, so why would she talk so foolishly, she replied, "Dreadful times are coming."

Poor Samuel scratched his chin. Now that he thought about it, he seemed to recall that she had not been sleeping well and had seemed agitated and distracted of late. In fact, just days before she had thrown scalding water at one of their children. The family all agreed this behavior was unexpected and abnormal—even for her. She had also been to visit their neighbor, John Moss, in recent days and had asked him to "look after" her husband. Mr. Moss didn't quite know what to make of this unusual request.

Despite Mercy's strange state of mind, what she did next was something few could have predicted.

In the early morning hours of June 23, 1691, Mercy's husband, Samuel Brown Sr., heard loud thumping sounds as though heavy blows were being dealt. He leapt from bed and made for the source, a nearby bedchamber. In the lamplight he saw his wife at the bedside of their seventeen-year-old son, Samuel Jr., her arms raised high. Mercy was engaged in striking the boy in the head with an axe.

The man shouted and rushed to her, yanking the axe from her grasp. He flung it away, and then he bent over the boy to see the extent of the damages. Samuel looked up in time to see his wife bearing down on them with the axe. He wrestled it from her once again and subdued her. Then he bellowed for help.

Samuel later learned that the attack had been planned. Sweet Mother Mercy had retrieved the axe from outside earlier in the evening and had hidden it from view in the folds of her dress. She had seemed rational to him, though perhaps a little distracted. This he attributed to her sporadic sleep of the previous days. Despite the man's efforts, his doting wife had delivered three vicious axe blows to his son and namesake, Samuel Brown Jr. The young man lingered six days before dying of his horrible head wounds.

Surprisingly, on October 12, 1691, Samuel Brown Sr. addressed the grand jury during the indictment hearing and pleaded in his wife's defense, explaining that she had no knowledge of her actions. He made a strong case for the fact that she had obviously become distracted, which in the parlance of the times meant she was mentally unstable. He urged them to not kill her but instead commit her to an asylum.

5

*Benjamin Tuttle swung from the gibbet in 1677 for cleaving his sister's head with an axe. He wasn't the only Tuttle sibling to favor that handy tool.*

The jury, however, remained unconvinced of her insanity. The judge thundered the facts of her commitment of "a most unnatural act," which he said had been instigated by the devil. He then said that for this, she should die. But Mercy was well regarded in the community, and numerous people of her acquaintance spoke on her behalf.

Luckily for Mercy Brown, the Crown-appointed governor of New England, Sir Edmund Andros, had recently been ignominiously booted back to England by a throng of peeved colonists. Because of this, a number of laws and their application were up in the air at the time of her sentencing, so Mercy evaded the hangman's noose.

Another of the Tuttle clan, the eighth child of William and Elizabeth, one Elizabeth—named for her mother (a move the elder Liz no doubt later regretted)—was, in keeping with family tradition, a bit of a scamp who had trouble showering her affections on just one man, even if that one man was her husband.

In retrospect, it seems that when Elizabeth Tuttle and Richard Edwards married on November 19, 1667, Dick really should have had an inkling of just what sort of woman he was tying the knot with, for she had been only too eager to break the law and had "lain with him" prior to their betrothal, a definite no-no for the times. So much so, in fact, that they were found out and were forced to pay five pounds to the county of Hartford's public fund.

Richard Edwards found after three months of marriage that Elizabeth was with child—but that it was not his. Elizabeth accused the father, one Mr. Randolph, before two judges, and her father, old William Tuttle, ended up raising the child. Poor Richard filed for divorce on July 2, 1689, basing his request on four points: "1: Her being guilty at first of a fact of ye same nature; 2: Her refusing me so longer together; 3: Her carage having been observed by some to bee very fond and unseemly to some other man than my self; 4: Her often commenting on other man with show or ye like worse he was worth a thousand of my self."

Richard made the mistake of mentioning that the other man might well have been one William Pitkin. And Pitkin, rightly or wrongly, defended himself and countered with a lawsuit of his own, claiming that Edwards's suit had been "derogatory of his honor."

Richard lost his plea for divorce and ended up living with her for nine years, during which time she abstained from allowing poor Richard any marital relations. In her defense, she was probably tired from dallying with men other than her husband.

After nearly a decade, Edwards could take no more of her philandering-and-then-withholding ways (now that's patience), and he lit out for foreign lands. He traveled by sea in an effort to give Elizabeth time to "repent." In truth, it gave her ample time to cavort. When Richard returned, it seemed to him that his absence had been the very thing their wobbly union needed, for they once again acted as husband and wife. But it wasn't long before Elizabeth slipped into her old ways, cheating on her husband over and over again . . . and again. Richard once more went to the courts and pleaded for divorce. But even with their two eldest children, Timothy and Abigail, testifying on behalf of their father and in opposition to their adulterous mother, his request was once again denied.

Richard explained how Elizabeth had, at times, threatened to kill him in his sleep. No one took his concerns seriously, however, until his wife's sister Mercy murdered her own son with an axe. And after all, they began to reason, Elizabeth's brother Benjamin had killed Elizabeth's sister Sarah, also with an axe. Hmm, maybe Richard was onto something. . . .

Two years passed and Edwards, no doubt tired from sleeping with one eye open, pleaded his case once again. Eventually his frantic request was considered and found not ungrounded. With the name Tuttle much in the news, the judges ruled "it is not within the compass of human power to deny him a divorce." No doubt each judge was counting his lucky stars that he hadn't married into the Tuttle clan.

Richard was most relieved, as he was keen to wed one Mary Talcott, a woman he'd been enjoying an extramarital affair with (one can hardly blame the guy). By all accounts, theirs was a stress-free and happy union that produced six sane children.

Oddly enough, of all the Tuttles of that generation, it is randy Elizabeth's line that begat a number of impressive Americans. Her grandson, by her son Timothy, was Jonathan Edwards, the Puritan who spurred into being the period of religious fervor called the Great Awakening. This Edwards was also known to be a bit overzealous in his preaching. Some say his fiery sermons bordered on . . . crazy.

Nutty or not, a number of this man's descendants would go on to be both extraordinary and infamous, though not always within the same person, as one might well suspect given the lineage behind them. They would hold impressive positions, including politicians, lawyers, judges, and doctors, with many notables among them, including Aaron Burr, third vice-president of the United States.

## CHAPTER 5

# Benedict Arnold:
## *From Hero to Traitor*

Though many Americans revile him today, few are certain why they say the name "Benedict Arnold" with a curl of the lip. Long before he became a sneered-at figure and his name synonymous worldwide with the word *traitor,* Benedict Arnold was on the fast track to becoming one of the greatest war heroes in US history. And then he became a turncoat and was found guilty of treason.

So why then paint Benedict Arnold with the jerk brush? Just because a person has proven himself filled with bravery doesn't mean he won't become traitorous. Bravery is defined as "courageous behavior or character," whereas a traitor is one who "betrays a friend, country, or principle." In Benedict Arnold, these traits existed in the same man, though not necessarily simultaneously.

For simplification of explanation, it is fair and useful to divide Arnold's life into two halves: pre- and post-treason. He was born on January 14, 1741, in Norwich, Connecticut. Though his was an old New England family of successful merchants, in the 1750s times grew tough for the Arnolds, and young Benedict (the third so named in his family) apprenticed to merchant cousins.

He was a quick study and soon, with the help of a family loan, set himself up as a merchant. Arnold excelled at his work and quickly gained a growing reputation in business circles as a bold, young risk taker. He purchased a fleet of three ships with a partner and traded in the West Indies. Shortly thereafter, and in defiance of the excessive British taxation brought on by the Stamp Act, he joined the Sons of Liberty, an underground group of men opposing exorbitant British taxes. As the revolution gathered momentum, Arnold soon rose to prominence as a reliable man who could get

*Benedict Arnold went from American war hero to reviled turncoat, then led British troops in ransacking and burning towns in his native Connecticut.*

things done. Arnold had also gained a reputation for being thin-skinned, and he often overreacted to perceived offenses that others might shrug off with a laugh.

In 1767, Arnold married Margaret Mansfield. The pair was quarrelsome and less than ideally matched; however, they managed to produce three sons. At the same time, and with the hounds of debt barking at his door, Arnold felt the revolution loom larger with each passing day.

As a commissioned captain in the Second Company, Connecticut Governor's Foot Guard, Arnold participated in early battles, notably at Lexington and Concord, then at the siege of Boston. When he recommended that the Massachusetts militia consider taking the British-controlled Fort Ticonderoga in New York, he was commissioned as a colonel and given the chance to spearhead the campaign. He led his men westward and arrived in Vermont, where he met up with Col. Ethan Allen and his Green Mountain Boys, a forthright if rough-cob outfit from the hills of Vermont.

In the early morning hours of May 10, 1775, Arnold was at the head of the charge when American troops burst through the gates at Fort Ticonderoga. No shot was fired in the raid, but Arnold, then thirty-four, forbade his fellow raiders from their intended task of looting their new British prisoners.

The Green Mountain Boys instead pillaged the fort and discovered the Brits' rum supply, in which they freely indulged. Soon their frustrations bubbled out in the form of drunken target practice . . . at Arnold. He managed to effect his escape without serious injury, but his by-the-book demeanor and tendency to look down his nose at others did not earn him friends at Ticonderoga. Instead, it earned him a rather large and long-lasting dose of enmity among his fellow soldiers, a lifelong trait to which he must have grown accustomed.

Among them, Arnold's haughty attitude clashed with equally strong-headed Allen and another officer, Col. James Easton, also of Connecticut, who grew weary enough of Arnold's superior demeanor to downplay in a follow-up report Arnold's significant role in capturing the fort. Benedict, justifiably incensed, challenged Easton to a manly duel, but Easton said thanks, but no thanks. Arnold should have left it at that, but instead he hit the man.

In a fit of pique, Arnold resigned his commission and discharged his troops, who promptly joined up with Easton. That must have gone over well with the embittered Benedict. Shortly thereafter, he learned of his wife's untimely death.

As if to make up for his repeated foibles and misfortunes, barely two months later, in August 1775, he accepted a colonel's commission from George Washington, who needed a strong tactical leader to spearhead an autumn expedition to attack Quebec City. Arnold suggested a route through unforgiving wilderness terrain in what would become the state of Maine. This would not be one of his wiser decisions. The treacherous trek was one for which the company was ill-prepared: Their boats were too heavy and swamped repeatedly, their food stores became sodden and useless, and they wobbled on the brink of starvation.

By the time Colonel Arnold's forces arrived in Quebec City in November, he had lost one-third of his 1,100 men to sickness and desertion. Arnold's eventual disastrous siege on Quebec City—along with the forces of Col. Richard Montgomery—cost Montgomery his life and Arnold the first in a series of debilitating injuries to his left leg. Still, in a move that he would repeat many times in subsequent battles, the wounded Arnold did his level best to rally his haggard troops. But it was too little, too late. They were routed from Canada. He would later redeem this loss by impressive commands at Montreal and on Lake Champlain, at the Battle of Valcour Island. Though in both instances the British won the day, Arnold's efforts and oversight were seen as key roles in delaying British advances.

Although he showed unflappable courage and impressive acumen on the battlefield, Arnold also could not seem to keep from annoying his fellow officers. While he gained a number of powerful allies in Congress, Arnold was a strong-willed man whose list of enemies included John Brown, an officer who publicly denounced Arnold and upbraided him in print for his bald-faced greed: "Money is this man's God, and to get enough of it he would sacrifice his country." More prophetic words about Arnold were never written.

And yet others praised him mightily. Consider Gen. George Washington's early assessment of him: "The merit of this gentleman is certainly great. I heartily wish that fortune may distinguish him as one of her favorites."

The words of Capt. Ebenezer Wakefield certainly spoke to Arnold's recognized strengths: "Nothing could exceed the bravery of Arnold. . . . He seemed the very genius of war." And Gen. Horatio Gates said of him, "Few men ever met with so many hairbreadth escapes in so short a space of time."

That might well be referring to any number of battles against the British at which Benedict Arnold repeatedly, battle after battle, refused to surrender and admit defeat. He held seven major commands throughout his American military career and participated in ten major battles of the Revolution. All told, he would have nine horses perish under him in battle.

Sadly for Arnold, his own significant contributions continued to be barely acknowledged, perhaps not in small part because of his prickly demeanor and constant wheedling for more pay. And yet Arnold kept on in this impressive-yet-insufferable vein until, in February 1777 he was once again passed over for promotion to the rank of major general, as he had been on a number of prior occasions. The Continental Congress instead chose to promote five officers, all Arnold's junior. Howling in rage, Arnold headed to Philadelphia to confront the powers that be.

Once again, General Washington intervened, in part to appease his complaining friend. He wrote a letter on behalf of the angry Arnold and others who had also been deserving of promotion but had been passed over in favor of political favoritism. Washington urged Congress to reconsider, else they "lose two or three other very good officers" should Congress continue to make appointments based on political favors and not necessarily merit.

In truth, Washington knew that in Arnold's case, at least, the decision had been based largely on the fact that the colonel was a prickly pear who made enemies easily.

None of this could keep Arnold from diving with gusto into the nearest fracas. At the battle of Ridgefield, Connecticut, on April 26, 1777, Arnold's horse was shot out from under him. The great wounded beast floundered, dropped, and pinned Arnold's already battered leg under the struggling horse. As a redcoat bore down on him, Arnold unsheathed his sword and fought the man in close combat, all the while struggling to free himself. He managed to dispatch his adversary and then hobbled to safety, only to secure another horse, then have that one, too, shot out from under him. Despite this, he led his men to a decisive victory that day.

In October 1777, at the Battle of Saratoga, Benedict Arnold came close to dying on the battlefield. The American forces were led by Gen. Horatio Gates—with whom Arnold butted heads time and again. Gates, for his part, did not like Arnold and not only undermined Arnold's orders to his men but repeatedly discredited Arnold's contributions to the cause at hand. Arnold fired scathing letters to Gates and angered the general enough that at Saratoga, Gates felt compelled to claim Arnold was engaged in insubordination. He relieved Arnold of his command, and the seething Arnold was ready to depart. Other officers intervened and convinced Arnold to stay. At least, they reasoned, they might be able to make use of his superior strategic and tactical skills. Lucky for all that they did, for Arnold's contributions are the stuff of legend.

On October 7, at Bemis Heights, stripped by Gates of his official command and confined to pacing in his tent, Arnold saw the American forces begin to waver and retreat. He could take it no longer and bolted from his tent, mounted his own horse, and, in a big-screen-movie moment, rallied the troops and led them back into the raging battle, musket fire whistling by him all the while. They fought on, rallied by this dynamic warrior, and followed him when he broke straight through the broken British lines. Soon, Arnold felt his horse faltering. The beast had been shot. He managed to drag himself out from under it and still he fought on. Then he took a ball to his already damaged left leg, now a splintered, shattered mess.

He continued to rally the men even as he was dragged from the battle, and the day's victory went to the Americans. Arnold was in agony but determined to keep his leg. Instead of allowing the doctors to amputate as they wished, he opted to have the shattered limb set. He did not know at the time that it would heal poorly (a full two inches shorter than the other leg), would become injured several more times in battle, and would trouble him greatly for the rest of his life. The battle had nearly cost Arnold his life, and yet it has long since been considered pivotal in turning the fortunes of the war to America's favor.

For his overwhelming contributions to that pivotal battle, the Continental Congress (begrudgingly) granted Arnold his long-sought promotion. He welcomed it, but the sting and deep-sunk barb of bitterness toward his perceived enemies within the Congress bloomed in his breast. He spent that following bitter winter at home in Connecticut, recovering from his extensive and slow-to-heal wounds.

In June 1778, following the British withdrawal from Philadelphia, George Washington appointed Arnold the military commander of the city. For anyone other than a man filled with bitterness toward his enemies, this position would seem to offer everything a military man could want. And for a while, it seemed to be just the ticket for Arnold. He also came to know one Peggy Shippen, the nineteen-year-old daughter of a Loyalist sympathizer.

Though two decades apart in age, the military hero and the fair maiden made quite a pair and wed the following year. Her father, Judge Edward Shippen, provided Arnold entrance into Philadelphia's high society, a set he craved to be part of. But moving in such circles comes with a price, and having a young wife used to living in the lap of luxury, surrounded by finery, also comes with a price—a high price. And Arnold soon found himself mired in debt.

Fortunately for Arnold, his position as the city's military commander afforded him the ability to funnel deals to his own private businesses. Those transactions were shady, to be sure, but not illegal. The aspect of his new life that would prove his ultimate undoing, however, were the friends that came with his new wife, a number of whom were British sympathizers. And one in particular, Maj. John Andre, was only too eager to help the debt-ridden military hero overcome his circumstances.

And thus came the budding of treason. The American war hero began negotiating with the British, sure that he had something to offer them, something with a price that would set him up once and for all in fine shape.

At the same time, Arnold's less-than-savory financial dealings were discovered, and he was called on the carpet once again before the Continental Congress. Specifically he was court-martialed, something he'd faced before. Unlike the previous outcome, however, this time he was found guilty of minor charges and suffered a public reprimand. He sulked and pouted and kicked at the dirt with his good leg and resigned his position as Philadelphia's military commander.

Washington let him stew for a few months and then suggested Benedict come back to active military service. Arnold had other plans, rubbed his sore leg, and countered with an idea he'd been cogitating on for some time: Why not give him command of the key New York military post at West Point? Washington rubbed his chin, considered Arnold's long and impressive service to his country, and agreed.

What Washington didn't know, however, was that Arnold had been quietly busy putting his affairs in order. He used his wife and her close Loyalist friends to pass encoded messages that detailed various American military secrets such as troop movement and logistical secrets. He sold his home and transferred various banking interests to British-controlled institutions. He also bumped up his asking price for turning over West Point to the British from 10,000 pounds to 20,000 pounds sterling and a commission in the English army. To this, the Brits readily agreed. Benedict was becoming a very, very bad boy.

He assumed command of West Point on August 3, 1780. With it, Arnold also wielded military control of all of Hudson Valley, a strategically placed plum for the British. He devised a plan in which British forces would attack West Point and its three thousand troops, an attack from which they would arise victorious. Arnold assured this outcome by reducing supplies (and selling them privately for personal profit) and poorly distributing his forces.

Reenter Maj. John Andre, who met with Arnold on September 21 near West Point. They made final arrangements and agreements, and then Andre departed. But his ship, the HMS *Vulture,* didn't make it far before it was attacked and driven back. Arnold supplied Andre with papers of safe passage, but the Brit was captured two days later at Tarrytown, New York. A search of his possessions turned up paperwork signed by Benedict Arnold. Specifically, there were items that spelled Arnold's downfall: encoded letters revealing troop positions and artillery details of West Point's defensive barriers—all handwritten by Arnold.

It was decided that Arnold, the region's commanding military officer, be informed only of Andre's capture. The capturing Americans withheld the fact that they had curious paperwork in Arnold's hand, opting instead to send it to General Washington, who as luck would have it, was engaged on military matters nearby.

On the morning of September 24, 1780, Arnold was informed that Andre had been captured and the paperwork he'd been carrying sent to General Washington. The implication was all too clear. With his treasonous actions all but revealed, Arnold knew he would soon be hung as a traitor. Arnold hadn't worked so long and so hard for it to all end at the end of a rope. He headed for the river, intending to somehow make his escape. If ever luck was with a man, it was with Arnold that day, for the HMS *Vulture* hove into view, seeking the whereabouts of Major Andre. Benedict Arnold flagged it down, hopped aboard, and made his escape as the incensed Washington and his men descended.

Though Arnold failed to turn over West Point, the British were still pleased to have the traitor in their midst and paid him a lump sum of 6,000 pounds sterling, an annual pension of 360 pounds, plus a commission as brigadier general. Washington, meanwhile, had Maj. John Andre hung.

Most chapters about Benedict Arnold end there, his exposed treachery seeming the ultimate crime. But Arnold seemed to never look back. He took to his new role like a duck to water. After having published a letter of explanation—not of apology—the next month in various British newspapers in New York City, called "To the Inhabitants of America," he explained his reasoning behind his traitorous behavior. And then, in control of 1,600 troops, he proceeded to descend on warehouses and munitions factories throughout Virginia, engaging in battle with Americans when need be, and being chased by them when outnumbered. Unsurprisingly, Arnold soon began making enemies among the British military officers, who were even less inclined than his American former fellow officers to put up with Arnold's bombastic ways.

Nonetheless, Arnold devised a plan to attack American forces in the stronghold harbor of New London in his home state of Connecticut. He led the raid, and soon, instead of just destroying the agreed-upon stocks of army supplies, fires raged out of control and burned most of New London to the ground. He then led a one-sided attack on Fort Griswold in Groton, Connecticut. The Americans suffered massive casualties. Of 150 men, 80 were killed, the rest imprisoned. So much for hometown pride.

Following the war, Arnold made his final move in 1782 to London, where he and Margaret "Peggy" Shippen Arnold failed to impress Whigs but did impress King George III and his Tories. Several years later, in 1787, Arnold and his two sons set up a mercantile business in Saint John, New Brunswick, but he moved back to London in 1791. He died there in 1801 and was buried at St. Mary's Church, Battersea, London, with no military honors. A century later, when the church underwent extensive renovations, Benedict Arnold's remains were put in an unmarked mass grave.

On his deathbed, Benedict Arnold is reported to have said, "Let me die in this old uniform in which I fought my battles. May God forgive me for ever having put on another." Hindsight, as they say, is twenty-twenty. Perhaps for a scoundrel such as Arnold, the past took on even sharper focus.

Why did such an impressive individual with so much going for him decide to turn against the side for which he so valiantly fought? The answers, as with so much in life, are both complex and simple: In short, Benedict Arnold was a bold man with a puffed-up sense of himself, not without reason, as we have seen. But he also had been passed over a number of times for promotions that he—and many others, including General Washington—felt he deserved. He was denied these promotions mostly because he was annoying, petty, vindictive, arrogant, and didn't have a problem reminding others of his valor in combat.

Couple these traits and gripes with a greed for acclaim and incessant and creeping debt, then toss in a lucrative possibility for making serious money—money that would help keep your pretty young wife happy and kept in fine style—and you have the makings of a traitor.

Ironically, Benedict Arnold was not the only high-profile traitor to emerge from the Revolutionary War. As General Washington said following Arnold's defection in September 1780, "Traitors are the growth of every country, and in a revolution of the present nature it is more to be wondered at that the catalogue is so small than that there have been found a few."

Benjamin Church was the first surgeon general of the US Army; his official title was "Chief Physician and Director General of the Medical Service of the Continental Army." He served in this capacity from late July to mid-October 1775. But Church was the original flip-flopper; in the years leading up to the war he alternately had supported the Whigs and had secretly been a Tory.

Despite the fact that he was an active participant in the Sons of Liberty movement prior to the war in Boston, he was found to have been offering secret information to British commander

Gen. Thomas Gage. One of Church's missives was a letter in cipher form that offered accounts of American forces and their locations outside Boston. In his correspondence, Church also professed loyalty to the Crown.

After his court martial at the hands of General Washington, who felt poorly used by the man, Church was jailed at Norwich, Connecticut, for a time, but he became ill. He was allowed to return to his native Massachusetts in May 1776, though still imprisoned. In 1778 he was released and left Boston on a ship bound for Martinique, but the ship was lost at sea. The British government paid his widow and family a pension.

Early in the twentieth century, historians discovered extensive further proof that Church had been in the employ of the British military, beginning in early 1775. He had been supplying military information for cash, which he needed in order to pay down his extensive debt.

Though not a New Englander, another traitor well worth mentioning was James Wilkinson, a high-ranking US Army commander. His questionable loyalty led to his resignation—twice—from the army. Despite the series of scandals in which he enmeshed himself, he twice held the position of commanding general of the US Army, and was also appointed the first governor of Louisiana Territory. Even after his death he continued to be a controversial figure.

Wilkinson was found to have been a double agent also in the employ of the Spanish Crown. It was not finally proven until 1854 that Wilkinson, in his guise as "Agent 13," had been working closely with the Spanish. Wilkinson's entire long and storied career as a US Army man was rife with treasonous activities. Sixty-five years later, no less a personage than Theodore Roosevelt, then New York's governor, said, "In all our history, there is no more despicable character." Well said, Ted.

## CHAPTER 6

# Barnett Davenport:
## *America's First Mass Murderer*

At the outset of this story, Barnett Davenport sounds like an upstanding guy—as a teen, he enlists in the Continental army to fight the British and ends up serving at both Valley Forge and Fort Ticonderoga. But these scant facts don't tell much of the foul man's story. Davenport led a troubling life in which his primary pursuits were lying, deserting, stealing, and, eventually, murdering. Was it his impoverished, work-filled childhood that made him into a human monster? Maybe the seeds of his future vileness were there at birth.

Barnett was the third of four boys born to John and Elizabeth Davenport of New Milford, Connecticut. From the age of seven, Barnett worked hard, long hours, as he was hired out by his father to local farmers. His chosen hobby, it seems, was thievery. He regularly filched items from the local populace, slowly drawing more attention to himself over the years. And by the time he reached twelve, by his own admittance, he felt the psychopathic urge to kill someone—anyone. He just needed to kill a person.

As a teenager, Davenport joined the Massachusetts army, not out of a burning desire to serve his country's cause, but because he was looking for a way to distance himself from the increasing scrutiny of the law, having recently been busy stealing horses.

When he joined the army, he did so under the false name of "Bernard." This would not be the last time he would use a false name. He deserted and then rejoined a different militia. He fought—one wonders how wholeheartedly—at Monmouth, under Washington at Valley Forge, and at Fort Ticonderoga under Benedict Arnold. The war dragged on and having had his bellyful of low wages, long hours, and hard work, Davenport up and deserted

*Barnett Davenport used a swingle such as this to bludgeon three of his victims to death. The others, two little boys, he burned alive.*

again. The nineteen-year-old made his way back to Connecticut and his home region.

Back home in Woodbury, he ran across Caleb Mallory, a local farmer, who took pity on the penniless, threadbare wretch and hired him on as a farmhand. In exchange for his labor, Davenport was given room and board. Other residents in the home included Caleb's wife, Elizabeth; an eight-year-old granddaughter, Charlotte; two grandsons, four-year-old John and six-year-old Sherman; as well as the Mallorys' daughter and son-in-law, the parents of the children.

The Mallorys were a well-liked family, hospitable and kindly. Too much so, as it turns out. Barnett Davenport ended up working for the family for two months before he decided he needed to kill them. It took that long for the need to commit murder to well up inside his psychotic mind until he had to satisfy it.

Was it the war that turned Davenport from a mere sociopath into a grade-A psychopath? Scholars in recent years have surmised that he might have come back from battle suffering some sort of post-traumatic stress. It's quite possible, though his activities and personal confessions prior to his time in the army suggest he was well on his way down that dark path, and that he had to work very hard to suppress those sinister urges.

Regardless of the motivation, in the dark late-night hours of February 3, 1780, Davenport crept into the bedroom of his employers, Elizabeth and Caleb Mallory. Caleb was in bed alone, his wife and eight-year-old granddaughter sharing a trundle bed close to the side. One can imagine the beast standing beside the bed, his decision having been made, his blood up, the lust of killing filling his very soul, his heart thumping in his chest, his hand gripping, relaxing, gripping the handle of the heavy wooden swingle (an implement used to thrash flaxseed), the other hand holding aloft a single lit candle.

With gritted teeth, Barnett Davenport raised the tool high, perhaps in his excitement clunking it against the room's low ceiling. He drove it down hard, hit the man once, and Caleb lashed out, shouting, then the candle flame guttered and died. This did not slow down the killer—he thrashed with the power of an enraged beast; again and again his arm rose and fell, the tool a bloodied, possessed thing.

The woman's screams mingled with the young girl's, then each voice dwindled to a bludgeoned gargling sound, then a hoarse whisper, before pinching out forever. The swingle splintered in Davenport's hand from the excessive pounding. He tossed it away and, snatching up the rifle leaning against the wall, continued pounding the bloodied trio with the gunstock. Satisfied that they were dead, he left the room.

It had taken more effort than he imagined it would take to kill them, and by the time he completed the dark deed, blood had spattered throughout the small chamber, soiled the bedding, dripped down the wall and off the ceiling, and, of course, it had sprayed all over him. The Mallorys' two young grandsons, John and Sherman, had left their bed and begun to cry, wondering what all the horrible noises might be, and why their grandparents weren't heeding their worried shouts. Davenport reassured the two youngsters that all would be well, and then he sent them back to bed.

He then hurriedly roamed the house, breathing hard and shaking, selecting what goods he could stuff in the sack he'd prepared just a short while before. A sound—groaning from Caleb—drew him back to the bedroom, where he slammed the butt of the musket downward again and again until he was sure Mallory was dead this time. But his own bloody clothes bothered him. They could attract attention and they were uncomfortable things, sticky, thick, and wet with blood, so he stripped out of them and donned a set of dry clothes belonging to Caleb Mallory.

Then he gathered up his loot and went from room to room, setting fires, burning the three people he'd savaged, and condemning to death the two living little boys trapped in the flames, screaming as their world erupted around them.

Much earlier in the evening, the parents of the three children had expressed their wish to visit friends that night. Davenport had convinced them that all would be well and had encouraged their visit away from the house. All this was no doubt part of Davenport's plan, as the parents, close in age to himself and used to a day's full labor, would have presented a formidable obstacle to his intended deed. It is probable that the young parents would have prevented him from carrying out the murders had they stayed home that night.

Barnett Davenport fled on foot and remained in hiding for six days. In that time, his younger brother, seventeen-year-old Nicholas, who lived nearby in the town of Torrington, was arrested and charged with the murders. Why? Because when Barnett had shown up two months before to ask for work at the Mallory place, he gave his name as "Nicholas." Now that's brotherly love for you.

Barnett was captured in Cornwall, hiding in a cave. When they hauled him to Newgate Prison, he learned that his younger brother, Nicholas, was also being held there, on the charges of being Barnett's accomplice. In an effort to free his innocent brother, the killer recanted his own earlier statement in which he'd claimed he had an accomplice. But the police said no-go, and stuck with their decision—even after they learned that Nicholas had had nothing to do with the crime. They still held him in custody, stating that he'd known about Barnett's desertion from the army and didn't come forward. They argued that had he done so, the murders would not have taken place.

At his arraignment in Litchfield, Barnett pled guilty and was sentenced to forty lashes, then death. The gallows had to be constructed anew, as hanging in Litchfield County was an uncommon occurrence. In fact, Barnett Davenport was but the fourth of five men to hold the distinction of being the guest of honor at such a necktie party in Litchfield County. He received his forty lashes and then was hanged by the neck until dead on May 8, 1780.

For his noncrime, Nicholas was given forty lashes and sentenced to serve life at Newgate Prison, a foul former copper-smelting facility. Before he was tossed in the clink, however, he was made to witness his brother's hanging. Not long after he was incarcerated, he escaped, was caught and dragged back, only to be released after serving two years.

This may have been the law's backhanded way of admitting it had falsely accused Nicholas of being his older brother's accomplice. Despite his granted freedom, he was made to promise that he would spend his life in New Milford. The damage to Nicholas's life had already been done—he died years later, a penniless pariah in his own community.

After the murders, Barnett Davenport admitted to the entire crime, and his lengthy, detailed confession was written down and transcribed. In the fourteen-page account, Davenport claims he had been obsessed with the very thought of killing the Mallory family for at least five days prior to doing so and had fought the urge to kill someone since roughly the age of twelve. Shortly thereafter, the confession was made available for sale to the public.

Barnett Davenport is considered America's first mass murderer—a person responsible for committing multiple deaths in a single incident. In his case, none of it was accidental, but all of it came about by chilling, premeditated design. And that makes it all the more horrific.

## CHAPTER 7

# Samuel Colt:
## *Brilliant Inventor, Shameless Huckster, Bullying Braggart*

Samuel Colt is widely regarded as the inventor of the revolver. However, that honor goes to another New Englander—Bostonian Elisha Collier who, in England in 1813, patented his flintlock revolver. The title of inventor of the first revolver in the United States, however, goes to New Hampshireman Harmon Fife, in 1835. What Samuel Colt did was *reinvent* the revolver to make it more efficient, hence the first "practical" revolver, for which he was granted a patent on February 25, 1836. And it is Colt's take on the form that would fast become the gun everyone on the frontier—and elsewhere—wanted.

Fife's design called for the user to cock the trigger guard, then squeeze the trigger to fire the ten-inch, seven-shot pistol. The downside? The revolving part, the cylinder, had to be rotated manually. Colt's primary improvement revolved the cylinder automatically, as the hammer was cocked—a most practical improvement, indeed.

But there are some who still maintain that Colt swiped the plans for Fife's primary contribution to the world of firearms. Even ol' Harmon went to his grave with doubt on his lips, literally, as his tombstone in North Pembroke, New Hampshire, reads:

*Here lies the man, never beat by a plan.*
*Straight was his aim and sure of his game.*
*Never was a lover but invented the revolver.*

And so a slight hubbub over the invention remains. But if that were the only shady undertaking Samuel Colt had been guilty of, his memory would have been a much less sullied thing. Alas, Samuel Colt was a busy fellow.

COLONEL COLT.

*Though a brilliant innovator, Samuel Colt was also equal parts egotist, huckster, and bully.*

He proved that a man could be capable of a whole lot more than one superlative in his lifetime. His impressive life story began in Hartford, Connecticut, in July of 1814 when Samuel, the fourth of five children, was born to Christopher and Sarah Colt. Samuel's mother died when he was but a lad of seven, and by age eleven Samuel was an indentured worker on a farm in Glastonbury, Connecticut.

There was no better place for a boy with a quick mind to grow up than in the Northeast during the burgeoning days of the Industrial Revolution, where he was surrounded by all manner of machinery and innovation. Colt found work in his father's silk mill, where the keen-minded youth paid careful attention to how the machines worked, and to how the various factory tasks were divided among the workers. It was also here that he first studied gunpowder, having befriended the factory's chemical specialist.

In addition to being possessed of an inquisitive mind, young Samuel was also a wayward rogue from an early age. Shortly after enrolling at Amherst Academy, he fired off a pistol and became mired in other episodes of petty trouble that would plague his school years. On July 4, 1829, he attracted a large crowd to local Ware Pond where he promised, as advertised on a handbill he'd passed out, to "blow a raft sky-high." It would be his first public display of underwater explosives, a pursuit he felt offered great promise.

The resultant blast splattered onlookers with a whole lot of water and mud, enough to enrage the gathered crowd. Luckily the giddy Colt, oblivious to the onlookers' anger, was spirited away by a concerned friend before the infuriated crowd could descend. The incident and a number of other similar experiments only fueled young Samuel's zeal for invention, for a life with purpose. He had specific interests, but they resided within a very broad spectrum of pursuits that included invention, improvement on others' inventions, and travel to exotic locales.

It was as a crew member of the ship *Corvo* that Colt spent spare time whittling a model of a pistol with a six-cylindered chamber that revolved—he'd been inspired by seeing the captain spin the ship's wheel. Once back on dry land, he had full-scale models made, and, armed with a letter of introduction from his father, the determined young man visited the head of the US patent office in Washington, DC. Colt's work was admired but thought to be too crude to risk a patent on.

Dismayed but undaunted, Colt spent two years working with three gunsmiths until he was satisfied that the designs were now up to snuff enough to risk another go at patent application. But the necessary gunsmithing didn't come cheap. Luckily Samuel Colt also showed ample sign of what would become his most endearing and infuriating trait—that of huckster showman and windbag raconteur.

Indefatigable as ever and dubbed "The Celebrated Dr. Coult of New York, London and Calcutta," he hit the popular traveling sales circuit, entertaining crowds up and down the East Coast with a laughing-gas show. Already aware of his abilities as a natural showman, Colt capitalized further on these abilities by incorporating with them the outlandish but alluring cries and sales patter of circus barkers and snake-oil hucksterism popular at the time.

Using nitrous oxide (laughing gas), he toured throughout the United States and into Canada, beginning his tour barking on street corners and eventually graduating to lecture halls, all the while impressing increasingly larger crowds with his burgeoning abilities as a showman. Colt soon realized that the public craved even more spectacle and pizzazz, so he partnered with a sculptor to create a stage show based on Dante's *The Divine Comedy*.

The resultant spectacle was a huge success and helped fund his abiding passion, and the direction where he felt his fortune lay, that of coming up with a truly practical revolver. He hired gunsmith John Pearson to help build his new prototype revolver, on which they worked together diligently to make it as close to perfection as possible before applying for a patent.

In August 1835, Colt traveled to Great Britain on advice from a US Patent Office employee (and former benefactor) to file for foreign patents. He was told that if he filed for a US patent first it would prevent him from obtaining certain foreign patents that could prove most lucrative later on. While in Europe, Colt visited France and England to file for patents there. He also managed to get married for the first time, to Miss Caroline Henshaw, in Scotland.

With a British patent secured, Colt traveled back to the States and, by February 1836, he had secured his long-sought US patent for a revolving gun, which soon enough would become his famous Colt Paterson. The patent also ensured that he had a monopoly on all revolving arms manufacture until 1857. By April, with the help of investors, he started the Patent Arms Manufacturing Company of Paterson, New Jersey.

Convinced that the only way to achieve true profitability in manufacturing was through the relatively new notion of an assembly line, wherein all the parts of his guns would be interchangeable, manufactured, and then put together by workers on the line, Colt plowed ahead. But the public wasn't quite ready for his products, it seemed. Largely due to national economic woes, by the end of 1837 Colt found himself sitting on a pile of one thousand brand-new firearms that no one seemed interested in buying.

Never one to pause for long, Samuel Colt headed out on the road in an effort to drum up sales at the local level. He reverted back to his street-corner patter, but sales refused to pick up. So he headed back to Washington, DC, where he met with President Andrew Jackson. The president was impressed enough to write Colt a note, praising the gun and offering his approval of it.

Armed with this fine endorsement, and his equally impressive chutzpah, Colt instigated Congress to grant him a demonstration for the US military. Unfortunately he neglected to scare up the necessary military purchase order, though he did impress the military enough to secure an order of up to seventy-five guns from the state of South Carolina. The order was later canceled when he failed to meet the promised deadline.

In Florida, the Seminole tribe had been causing quite a scuffle, and the state placed an order of one hundred guns from Colt to help fight them. These guns were largely well received, though the design so differed visually from previous models the soldiers had been using that they began dismantling the guns out of curiosity, and in the process they broke numerous parts. But in another instance of Colt making lemonade from lemons, he redesigned the revolvers, exposing the hammer and improving his design.

Yet for all his successes, Colt's guns still didn't sell well. Payment for the guns used in Florida never materialized, and Colt slipped into bankruptcy in 1842. Soon he was forced to close his Paterson, New Jersey, plant. But as much as he wanted the world to think so, the blame can't be laid entirely on the fact that the guns didn't sell.

It seems Samuel Colt contributed significantly to his company's financial woes by overspending in a number of ways. He indulged himself in extravagant wardrobes and bought lavish gifts for people he wished to impress—some of whom were potential clients, some of whom were ladies of his acquaintance. He wined and dined them to such an extent that twice his accountant was forced to cut him off from his own company's expense account. Colt also often failed to pay his gunsmith and conveniently neglected those pesky bills for raw materials and supplies.

Colt may have had to close up shop, but he was hardly lazing about. He worked on a number of inventions that held promise, though none achieved anything more than modest success. These included batteries for use underwater, as well as underwater mines for naval harbor defense. He also worked to correct the long-term problem of wet powder and nonfiring rounds by developing a waterproof cartridge using tinfoil. He struck up a friendship with another well-known Samuel—Samuel Morse of Morse code fame. The men collaborated, and Colt's underwater batteries proved invaluable to Morse's telegraph-cable development.

In 1847 came the Mexican War and with it a sudden demand for Colt's pistols. The Texas Rangers, in fact, had been using Colt's pistols and finding them so effective that Gen. Zachary Taylor sent Capt. Samuel Walker back East in person with an order for more. But Colt had none of the models on hand. He even resorted to advertising for one in newspapers but couldn't wait, so he ended up building a new model from scratch, augmenting his old design with suggestions for improvements from Walker.

What they came up with is the stuff of frontier legend. No longer were Colt's pistols passed over by the army for being too fragile for military use (an early claim). This new .44 caliber pistol weighed in at five pounds and measured fifteen inches. And Texas Rangers loved it, claiming it could drop an enemy at a quarter mile over flat ground. It also held six shots instead of Colt's previous five-cylinder design, earning it the designation as the world's first six-shooter.

In 1849, Colt's revolvers became a runaway hit. Coupled with the recent payoff of his creditors, his firm once again began making money, this time hand over fist. The Pocket Revolver became its biggest seller to date—just in time for argonauts venturing westward in search of gold: 325,000 of the handy handguns sold. All these sales worked wonders for Colt's wallet, too, for they launched a string of government contracts that continued for many decades.

For a time his guns were made in Whitneyville, Connecticut, at the plant of Eli Whitney Jr., maker of cotton gins and guns. Colt wasted no time in beginning construction of his own facility in Hartford, Connecticut. He hired his old friend, Elisha Root, an engineer of considerable and growing repute, to oversee the design and construction of the new armory as well as its manufacturing line. Colt concentrated on what he did best, designing new firearms and acting as chief publicity maven for the growing company.

He designed and manufactured firearms in a variety of sizes, weights, and calibers that proved popular with the US military, sailors, Pony Express riders, plainsmen, dandies, gamblers, gold seekers, and more. Colt even opened a plant in London to cater to the arms trade generated by the Crimean War.

By 1856 Samuel Colt was a millionaire, and he employed hundreds of people at his ever-expanding factory. In its first quarter century in operation, Colt Manufacturing cranked out four hundred thousand revolvers. As a pioneer in the practice of mass production of interchangeable parts, and as the first manufacturer to use them in an assembly-line setting, he was able to fulfill huge contracts that other makers were unable to even consider. His success in this area emboldened all manner of manufacturing in various other fields.

In return he ran the place as though it were a military organization and he the general in charge. Much of Colt's continued success came about because of his early and repeated use of bribery and threats (legal and otherwise), and with the legal (barely) monopolization of the revolver trade.

But as soon as his patent ran out in 1857, the gravy years ground if not to a halt, then certainly to a slower speed. All manner of competitors flooded the firearms marketplace, including Henry, Sharps, and Smith & Wesson. But Colt rose to the challenge—and took full advantage of looming civil unrest. The Union army gobbled up his new 1860 Army model, a redesigned version of the older models. It became the Union's standard sidearm during the Civil War.

Until war was actually declared, Colt sold arms to both sides, including two thousand guns in one famous sale to a Confederate agent in 1861. He even entertained the idea of building a manufacturing facility in the South. Curiously, Colt's only opposition to slavery was that it made no economic sense to him. He regarded slavery as an inefficient use of manpower. Morally he was not necessarily opposed to it, and politically he was no fan of President Lincoln.

While legal, his 1861 sale of two thousand revolvers to the Confederate army raised eyebrows and the ire of the mighty Northern press. And it was this long-standing practice of Colt's that convinced people once and for all that he was out for number one, in it for the money and not the side in a fight.

A number of powerful newspapers such as the *New York Times* and the *Hartford Daily Courant* accused him of being a traitor. Colt turned to the state of Connecticut once more and demanded he be made a colonel. The resultant unit, the 1st Regiment Colts Revolving Rifles of Connecticut, was little more than a balm for the wounded ego of this wealthy resident. Colt saw it as his own little army of highly trained men, each armed with his unique revolving rifle. Alas his commission lasted little more than a month, and his dream regiment never made it out of the starting gate.

As a born salesman, Samuel Colt was both shameless and innovative in his pursuit of publicity, and it has been said he would do anything to make a sale. He famously persuaded the governor of Connecticut to give him the honorary title of lieutenant colonel in the Connecticut militia so that he might gain audiences with foreign courts and dignitaries who otherwise would not meet with private citizens.

And when he did meet with famous heads of state, kings, and others, he presented them with personalized, richly appointed, engraved revolvers in special one-of-a-kind presentation cases. He also snagged numerous highly coveted government contracts because he greased political wheels with cash and gifts of lavishly engraved revolvers with pearl and ivory handgrips to politicians and heads of state.

One such instance saw Colt make a gift of a gold-inlaid revolver to the sultan of the Ottoman Empire. Knowing that the Russians were the sultan's enemies, Colt informed him that the Russians had bought guns. So the sultan, not to be outdone by the Russians, placed an order for five thousand Colt revolvers. What Colt didn't tell the sultan is that he had presented the Russian leader with a similar gift and sales pitch, and it worked on the Russians, too, who also placed a large order for pistols.

He commissioned original artwork from painter George Catlin, instructing him to show the heroes of the piece plainly using Colt weapons. He was also revolutionary in his use of the press; not only did he run multiple advertisements in single issues of publications but he commissioned a twenty-nine-page illustrated supplement to a single issue of *United States Magazine.* A true visionary, he was sure that his efforts and expenses would be well repaid with residual sales—and he was correct.

He carried the practice of subtle manipulation of the press to disputable heights, encouraging positive press about his products by making a gift of a free revolver to writers who penned pieces that lauded the Colt handgun and slagged the competitors' products.

Soon his signature appeared on his handguns, advertising, and publicity pieces, enough so that he had his signature trademarked. He also pioneered the use of celebrities to endorse his weapons and is said to be the first manufacturer to use the phrase "new and improved" in advertising his wares. So ubiquitous worldwide has his surname become that the French word for "revolver" is Le Colt. And in the United States, even today people often refer to pistols as "Colts." A catchphrase still bandied about in the press states that "God made man, but Samuel Colt made them equal."

Oddly enough, the Peacemaker, the gun for which his company is arguably best known, didn't come out until long after his death, in 1873.

In his late thirties, a multimillionaire living life on a large and lavish scale, Colt drew up plans for a massive expansion of his manufacturing facility in Hartford. He required hundreds more acres to accommodate the enormity of his vision, and he acquired them by gobbling up some 250 lowland acres along the Connecticut River. He intended to make the manufacturing facility the best in the world, hiring only the best designers, machinists, and others. He planned to build housing, stores, libraries, gardens, and more for his employees—all to accommodate the manufacture of his firearms.

He was thwarted several times in his efforts by people who refused to sell their land to this juggernaut of commerce, though in one instance, even his usual routine of bullying and bribery failed to get him what he wanted. He resorted to manipulation of the press in an effort to uproot the holdout, but even derogatory media didn't work. So Colt rubbed his hands together and installed a brothel right across the street from the holdout's abode. This tactic worked, and Colt got his land.

And on the frequent occasion when he demanded too much from the local community and the people told him no, a word he was not used to hearing, Colt repeatedly threatened to close up shop lock, stock, and barrel, and move to a different state. That always won the argument.

The result, completed in 1855, was Coltsville, the largest private firearms and munitions factory in the world. In return for ten-hour workdays and one-hour lunch breaks, his male workers received top pay. Colt's female workers, however, were paid as little as he could get away with. He often hired unmarried immigrant women to handle the most dangerous of tasks—fulfillment of gunpowder and ammunition orders.

On June 5, 1856, Samuel Colt married Elizabeth Jarvis, a society belle a dozen years younger than he (he was forty-one, she twenty-nine), then immediately decamped to Europe for six months. On his return, he began construction of Armsmear, a massive, ostentatious mansion overlooking Coltsville. The couple lost four children, the oldest dying at three. Another son, Caldwell, outlived his father, but only to age thirty-five, when he died of tonsillitis.

Colt's jerkiness is more of the accumulated variety. That he was a brilliant man is not in question. Stepping on a lot of people, publicly and privately, however, is not usually considered good form. Though he conducted himself wolfishly professionally, it was how Samuel Colt conducted himself in his private life that still makes eyebrows rise.

Though he never admitted to it publicly in his lifetime, Samuel Colt had fathered a son with his first wife, Caroline Henshaw, whom he married in 1835 while procuring European patents. Samuel had since decided that because his fortunes had changed and he was now a big wheel, Henshaw was not of sufficient quality to be the wife of such a prominent industrialist.

Instead, in an effort to keep her from revealing the truth—and legitimizing the child—Samuel encouraged his brother John to marry Henshaw, whom Samuel had by then divorced. John and Caroline married on the morning of November 14, 1842, the very day that John Colt was to be hung for the murder of a man he had killed a year earlier with a hatchet. Later that day, John Colt stabbed himself in the heart and died before he could be hung.

On the death of his brother, Samuel assumed financial responsibility of his and Henshaw's son, put him through private schools, and gave him a generous allowance. But he never admitted paternity of the youth. The boy's name? Samuel Colt Jr.—even though Senior referred to him forever after in correspondence, and in quotes, as his "nephew."

When Samuel Colt died in 1862 of gout at the young age of forty-seven, Colt's estate was valued at roughly $15 million ($350 million today). He left it to his thirty-five-year-old widow and three-year-old son Caldwell. His first son, Samuel Caldwell Colt, received the equivalent in today's dollars of $2 million. His second wife protested this in court, but young Samuel produced a marriage certificate that proved his claim as "nephew." In truth, as first-born he should have been heir to the full Colt Manufacturing Company.

Colt's widow, Elizabeth, went on to ably run—and continue to promote in as grand a fashion as her husband—Colt Manufacturing Company for many years. And just as her husband is regarded as one of America's preeminent inventors and trailblazing manufacturers in so many ways, and a brilliant mind, so she is long remembered as a benefactress whose generosity to Hartford, Connecticut, is still appreciated today.

So if Samuel Colt was such an amazing man, an inventor of noted repute, what made him so jerky? Was it his shameless hucksterism? His self-aggrandizing manner? Hardly—and though these traits can rub folks the wrong way, a lot of Americans have gotten a lot of mileage out of them. What qualifies him as a jerk are the many shady ways in which he conducted himself professionally and personally.

Samuel Colt was a ruthless competitor, stopping at nothing to land a contract and at the same time smear his competition. He lied, failed to pay bills, treated other peoples' work as his own, intentionally created monopolies, and prevented others from prospering. Such cold, heartless business practices could just as easily have been dispensed with, and his reputation for all his invention and talent would be all the greater for it, rather than suffering the tarnish with which his misdeeds have instead colored it.

## CHAPTER 8

# John Endecott:
## *Hotheaded Puritan, Intolerant Tyrant*

Puritans began to establish settlements and populate southern New England—Massachusetts, Connecticut—beginning in 1620. Hardworking, industrious, and pious, these extreme Protestants believed that the Church of England had gone soft. They wanted simpler, more straightforward, and stricter forms of worship, most notably hard censorship of pleasurable pursuits—and they were willing to force their views on anyone who got in their way. Grim and dogged in driving to ground anyone exhibiting what they considered witchlike traits and relentless in their pursuit of anyone not adhering to their beliefs, most notably Quakers, Puritans left a lasting, painful scar on New England history.

In what has been called the Great Migration, a period between 1630 and 1642 saw twenty thousand Puritans settle in Massachusetts. They were preceded in 1628 by an advance group that included, among other notables, one John Endecott, soon to be known as a Puritan among Puritans.

Long before he was a hotheaded religious zealot in the New World, John Endecott was a hotheaded young man back in England. He was born in approximately 1600 in or near Devon, England. Details of his early life, including the names of his parents, are unknown. What is known is that he was intelligent, spoke French, and may have had some military experience as well as experience in medicine. Smugness, intolerance, and disdain for others he picked up along the way.

In March 1628, he was chosen by the privately funded Plymouth Council for New England, an outfit concerned with establishing colonies in North America, to lead the first foray of what was known as the New England Company for a Plantation in

*Quakers seeking freedom from religious tyranny did not find it under John Endecott, Puritan and longtime governor of Massachusetts Bay Colony, who advocated torture and death for members of the peace-seeking group.*

LIBRARY OF CONGRESS

Massachusetts. Endecott and fifty others set sail on June 20, 1628. They were not the first to settle in the region, as others of an earlier expedition were already there, in addition to the nearby, well-established Plymouth Colony. Endecott's settlement became known as Salem the following year. It was also given a royal charter, and with it, Endecott became the first governor of the Massachusetts Bay Colony.

Over the following difficult winter, a number of people died, including Endecott's first wife, Anne Gower, cousin of the company's London-based governor. Endecott married again (either once or twice more, the records are unclear on this fact) to a woman named Elizabeth, who bore him two sons. It is also suspected that he fathered a child prior to leaving for New England, but records of this product of his youth remain sketchy.

Early in the colony's establishment, Endecott showed the first signs of what would later become his flaming religious intolerance. As governor of the company, Endecott strutted as if he ruled completely—and it seems he did wield considerable power. He conflicted with Thomas Morton, a man whose nearby failed colony of Wessagusset instigated anger in Endecott, who was annoyed that Morton allowed celebration at his colony. A maypole at the settlement so offended Endecott's Puritan sensibilities that he ordered it immediately dismantled. He also sent the leaders of another group of would-be settlers packing back to England when they dared to try to establish a non-Puritan-based church.

By 1630, religious disagreements arose between leading factions of the church at the time, Separatists and their opposites, Nonconformists. Endecott went against his fellows by offering protection for Separatist Roger Williams, who would go on to found Providence, Rhode Island, after being forced to flee from Salem.

This period of religious tension coincided with Endecott's continued rise to power in the New World and allowed Endecott's emerging strident religious intolerance to flourish. He was in a position to influence and exert his personal interpretation of his own thinly defined but strict views of Puritanism on everyone he could. He raged long and loud about the need for women to dress as the very model of modesty, going so far as to request they wear face veils while attending church. But he did not limit his prudish opinions to the fairer sex.

Men, he determined, should not be allowed to wear their hair long, as outlined in a lofty statement written by Endecott in May 1649: "Forasmich as the wearing of long haire after the manner of Ruffians and barbarous Indians, hath begun to invade new England contrary to the rule of gods word . . . Wee the Magistrates who have subscribed to this paper . . . doe declare and manifest our dislike and detestation against the wearing of such long haire."

He seemed to take particular relish in banishing individuals who dared to outwardly worship differently than Puritans. In 1644 he convicted three men of being Baptists, referred to them as "trash," and gave them the choice of a fine or a whipping. Endecott, still unsatisfied with this lenient treatment, sought harsher punishment for them. Two of the men were freed on payment, but one was whipped, though Endecott felt they had all "deserved death."

Endecott really warmed to his work when nonconformists crossed his path. One of his most famous acts occurred in 1634, when he publicly held aloft the English flag and slashed it with his saber, because at the time the flag bore St. George's Cross, which represented the papacy. For this, Endecott was censured by his fellow administrators who felt that the act was far too rash. (Even among Puritans he was hardcore!)

They were acting prudently, given that the colony was under the close scrutiny of the Crown's Privy Council, a board examining the budding colony's progress that would help decide if it deserved to retain its royal charter from King Charles I.

As punishment for his bold, hotheaded actions, Endecott was barred from holding public office for the full year of 1635. For a man such as John Endecott, who equated his public positions with godliness, piousness, and power, all things he craved in great quantity, that year—the only one in his New World life in which he failed to hold public office—must have been a long, torturous time for him.

All of this intolerant behavior was but practice and led up to his largest and longest-lasting Puritanical pursuit. In 1636, what should have been an exploratory expedition to find out the guilty parties behind an Indian raid on a trader's ship became instead the opening volley of violence in what would quickly become the Pequot War. This four-year episode resulted in many deaths and enslavements—seven hundred—and in the near annihilation of the Pequot Indian tribe.

On July 20, 1636, the ship of trader John Oldham, from Massachusetts, was overrun and looted by Indians on Block Island. The English blamed the Narragansett tribe, but the Narragansetts blamed the Pequot tribe, who had been less willing thus far to behave as the English and other local tribes wanted them to.

The Pequot were a more warring bunch, busy expanding their territory, and in the process their enmity earned the fear and anger of the English colonists.

Massachusetts governor Henry Vane turned to John Endecott, a high-ranking military officer, with orders that he take ninety men to Block Island to get to the root of the matter. But his orders against the Indians were explicit: Endecott was to kill the men and capture the children and women. He and his men landed, and though they met little resistance—and lost many potential prisoners because the children and women hid—the English nonetheless made a feast of it, spending two days looting, and destroying crops and villages. Endecott claimed fourteen dead Pequot, but the Indians claimed only one of their number had been killed. The real initial damage was the theft of their winter food stores and the burning of their villages.

Next Endecott's men were ordered to confront the Pequot tribe at their stronghold near the mouth of the Thames River on the mainland. When they arrived there, Endecott demanded reinforcements from the English settlement at Saybrook, much to the dismay of its leader, Lion Gardiner. The man had little choice and begrudgingly accompanied Endecott's forces on a raid intended in part to destroy the Pequot's food stores.

The Pequot greeted their ship with smiles that quickly faded when they heard Endecott's demands: the Pequot warriors who had killed the traders be turned over, significant monetary payment be rendered, and a number of Pequot children had to be offered to them as hostages. The Pequot emissary nodded and headed back to his village to deliver these ultimatums. But Endecott was an impatient man and would not be kept waiting. He ordered his armed—and armored—men ashore. Soon the emissary returned, wringing his hands and explaining that tribal leaders were not there. Endecott was having none of it, and the inevitable attack began.

Despite Endecott's zeal for revenge and blood, the Pequot villagers escaped. He satisfied himself by repeating what he had done to the Pequots on Block Island—he rode hard and roughshod, destroying their village and stealing their stored crops, condemning them to a winter of starvation.

Endecott set sail with his initial group of men, plus the spoils of the raids: much foodstuffs and many captive Indians from the first raid. He also left behind Lion Gardiner and his men, who soon enough felt the full sting of the Pequot warriors' wrath—they were attacked and barely escaped with their lives. Endecott, meanwhile, sailed blithely homeward, doing what he did best: leaving behind a trail of woe and smoking wreckage.

But back home, Endecott was called on the carpet. Colonists were filled with rage at what they regarded as Endecott's "heavy-handed provocation." They were convinced an Indian war was brewing, and, as they lived in relative peace and close proximity to the now-enraged tribes, the colonists feared for their lives.

Their fears were well founded: As early as April of the next year, 1637, a number of communities were attacked by the Pequot and their allies. The Pequot War was underway. And it raged on, resulting in a steady attrition of the Pequot people. At the Mystic Massacre, on May 26, 1637, of roughly seven hundred Pequot Indians, only fourteen survived; seven of them were taken as prisoners, seven escaped.

Within months, the remaining straggling bands of refugee Pequot were hunted down by English and by Mohegan and Narragansett warriors until, on September 21, 1638, when the Treaty of Hartford was signed, only two hundred Pequot remained, most of them elderly, women, and children. They were forcibly disbanded, sold into slavery, or assimilated into other tribes and never again officially recognized as Pequot.

And where was John Endecott in all this? After he kicked off the proceedings with his brutal raids, he sat out the rest of the war. He was rewarded for his efforts in 1641 by once again becoming elected to public office, this time as deputy governor of the Massachusetts Bay Colony.

Endecott's ham-handed actions of 1636 are regarded now as a major mistake in dealing with the Indians, an overreaction to what could have been handled diplomatically to the satisfaction of all parties involved. But it turned out very much the opposite, and Endecott continued to rule—indeed, his longest days in public office were ahead of him.

John Endecott's crowning achievement, and the one that alone would have earned him the crown of "King of Jerks," occurred when he was forced to deal with a particular brand of religion he openly despised: Quakers. Unfortunately for these religious free-thinkers, Endecott's hatred was shared by many colonists.

In reaction to Oliver Cromwell's rise to power in England in the 1650s, a number of small but thriving freethinking religious communities fled England and headed to America, an alleged safe haven for religious pilgrims—the Quakers being the most notable group among them. The first Quakers to arrive in America, in 1656, were given the heave-ho back and were forced to return to where they came from by Endecott's underling, Richard Bellingham. Soon enough more arrived, and Endecott wasted no time in shunting them to prison to await a biased trial over which he would preside.

One brave Quaker woman, Mary Price, wrote to Endecott and requested a meeting in an effort to explain her religious views. She was nothing if not optimistic in her hopes of changing the pious Puritan's mind about his continued deportation of Quakers. Her efforts did not succeed, and she and her fellow Quakers soon found themselves back on the high seas.

Endecott's firm hand and open hatred of such "ungodly" people resulted in giving all public officials the right to oust any Quakers found in their jurisdictions. But they did not count on such a massive influx of Quakers landing on New England shores. Never one to allow himself to be overwhelmed, Endecott and his fellow New England Confederation (an alliance of Puritan colonies) cohorts came up with stricter measures to deal with this new scourge against Puritanism. By the mid-1650s, Endecott's religious intolerance was so developed—or rather, stunted—that he ordered that Quakers be put to death should they refuse to accept his imposed banishment from the colony.

Quakers who returned to a place from which they had been previously banished suffered the punishment of having their ears cut off. A third return qualified them for a treatment in which their tongue be "bored through with a hot iron." Soon, however, death became de rigueur for a third offense, at which time the accused must also "plainly and publicly renounce their said cursed opinions and devilish tenets."

Criticized by the public for being harsh, the law was amended later in 1658 so that second offenders in Massachusetts could keep their ears, but they were also given the death penalty. The following year three Quakers, two men and a woman, were convicted and set to receive this harsh retribution. The men were hanged, but the woman, Mary Dyer, was reprieved.

Not one for backing down, the next year, in 1660, Dyer defied orders and returned to the Massachusetts Bay Colony and was imprisoned. She underwent harsh questioning by Endecott and his cronies, and in the end she refused to tolerate their offer— permanent banishment from the colony. She also fervently refused to recant her Quaker beliefs. So Endecott ordered Mary Dyer to hang for her beliefs, and she swung from the gallows on June 1, 1660. The following year another Quaker was hanged. Since then, the four hanged Quakers have come to be known as the Boston Martyrs.

Colonists of the time were largely intolerant of Quakers, but even they regarded Endecott's laws as harsh. After extended complaining, much to his dismay Endecott was forced to alter his laws so that a fifth offense earned Quakers death.

Though it would take two decades, by 1684 one of the reasons cited for revocation of the colonial charter would be intolerance of religious dissenters, including Quakers. Too little, too late for the Boston Martyrs.

John Endecott continued to serve the public until his death at the approximate age of sixty-five on March 15, 1665. His remains can be found at tomb 189 in the Granary Burying Ground, Boston's third-oldest cemetery.

The Endecott name (spelled variously with an "e" or an "i") continued on throughout New England, and several of the intolerant tyrant's descendants have held high political and military office. The ship, *Governor Endicott,* was named for him, as is Endicott College in Beverly, Massachusetts. And Endicott Rock, New England's oldest public monument, sits at what was, in 1652, the assumed headwaters of the Merrimack River.

Despite the various namesakes, monuments, and memorials, later years would not be kind to John Endecott. Famous New England authors including John Greenleaf Whittier, Henry Wadsworth Longfellow, and Nathaniel Hawthorne all took turns at immortalizing the zealot in an unkind, though wholly deserved light.

In the poem "Cassandra Southwick," about a long-suffering Quaker under Endecott's thumb, Whittier wrote, "And on his horse, with Rawson, his cruel clerk at hand, / Sat dark and haughty Endicott, the ruler of the land."

Longfellow named one of three poems in his collection *New England Tragedies* after Endecott. "John Endicott" detailed the 1661 trial of Wenlock Christison, the last person to be condemned to death in the Massachusetts Bay Colony for being a Quaker.

Finally, in his story "The Gentle Boy," about the six-year-old son of executed Quaker Mary Dyer, Hawthorne provided an even less endearing description of Endecott as "a man of narrow mind and imperfect education, and his uncompromising bigotry was made hot and mischievous by violent and hasty passions; he exerted his influence indecorously and unjustifiably to compass the death of the enthusiasts and his whole contact, in respect to them, was marked by brutal cruelty."

## CHAPTER 9

# Masterminds of the Salem Witch Trials: *A Horde of Hysterics*

In a strange period of mass hysteria that gripped Massachusetts from February 1692 to May 1693, dozens of people were rounded up in the middle of the night, during daylight working hours, in the fields, on the roads, sitting down to a meal with their families—more than 150 people in all suffered the stress and humiliation of arrest and imprisonment on suspicion of witchcraft. And it was all because a couple of little girls played a childish game that was taken to extremes by adults who should have known better.

The courts convicted twenty-nine of these citizens of the bizarre, unsubstantiated crime. Of the convicted, fourteen women and five men were hung for being witches, and one was pressed to death with stones. Five more never made it out of prison. Oddly enough, despite all the pop-culture blather to the contrary, no one accused of witchcraft in Salem was burned at the stake.

How did this shameful period of mass hysteria come about, and why was it allowed to rage unchecked for as long as it did? This appalling but fascinating period came to be known as the Salem Witch Trials, a slight misnomer, since they actually took place throughout the surrounding region and included the towns of Salem Village, Ipswich, Andover, and Salem Town.

By the latter half of the seventeenth century, squabbling and backbiting among the inhabitants of the towns of Salem Village (now Danvers) and nearby Salem Town, in addition to other local villages, became increasingly heated. Land ownership, property-line disputes, petty vandalism among neighbors, and a variety of other hot-button topics and troubles kept tempers percolating.

*The writings of Cotton Mather, Puritan minister, more so than any other influence, fanned the flames of superstition resulting in the mass madness of the Salem Witch Trials.*

Another sore spot not allowed to heal was the position of minister of Salem Village. Mostly due to their own scrimping ways—they didn't pay what they'd promised—the villagers lost three ministers in little more than a decade. By the time the congregation settled on Samuel Parris as its first ordained minister, villagers had, it seemed, learned their lesson, and they were prepared to pay a decent sum to keep him in the position. Unfortunately for many locals, Parris turned out to be a fomenter of trouble, a muckraker who intentionally looked for what he called "iniquitous behavior," defined as anything *he* didn't feel the church would approve.

In those days, local ministers, and especially those who had been ordained, held a lofty social status, second only to certain politicians. And since they represented the word of God in corporeal form, the words of ministers and other figures of the cloth tended to carry much authority, a power Reverend Parris was only too eager to wield. He routinely forced members of his congregation to endure public penance, sometimes for a sleight as minor as smiling at the wrong time.

Any act resembling paganism, such as dancing, celebration of Christmas and Easter, and any music other than hymns sung without musical accompaniment, was forbidden. Children had a rough time of it, too, as games and toys were considered frivolities. The only fun people were allowed came in the form of twice-weekly meetings at the church, where they had to endure Parris's three-hour sermons.

Rev. Cotton Mather, a minister from Boston and son of Increase Mather, the influential Puritan minister, can take much of the credit for inciting the fervor that resulted in the Salem trials. In 1689 he published a book titled *Memorable Providences Relating to Witchcrafts and Possessions,* in which he described the fits experienced by the children of Bostonian John Goodwin. These spastic episodes were alleged to have been caused by Goodwin's neighbor, accused of witchery when in fact she was merely a disgruntled old washerwoman who, having grown tired of local children soiling the laundry over which she labored, shouted at them to leave her alone.

But Mather, a fervent believer in the existence of witchcraft, documented the various afflictions suffered by the children, among them "the disease of astonishment," manifestations of which were neck pains, odd shouts, birdlike arm flapping, and falling over in a limp heap.

The popularity of Mather's work influenced the girls in the household of pious Reverend Parris. In January of 1692, the reverend's nine-year-old daughter, Betty, and her eleven-year-old cousin, Abigail Williams, began to behave like animals, crawling instead of walking. They screamed, hurled objects, and convulsed in spasms, at times completely out of control in their epileptic-like seizures. The girls were examined by doctors, who found nothing wrong with them medically. But soon, other young women of the village began acting in a similar manner.

Three women were arrested and charged with afflicting four young girls of the village. Sarah Good, Sarah Osborne, and a black slave named Tituba were the first people formally accused of witchcraft in Salem. A survey of those charged with the crime reveals from the start a stacked deck. These three women each were nonconformists, according to the Calvinist views of the villagers.

The first, Good, was a destitute beggar; Osborne was not much of a churchgoer and had also done other things of which her fellow community members didn't approve, such as marrying an indentured servant. The last, Tituba, was a slave whose physical appearance had already set her apart from everyone else in the community. But Tituba also had been a favorite among the girls, an older sister of sorts, who told them folktales and stories from her native Haiti.

Soon the fingers of accusation also pointed inward, to people within the church itself, among them Martha Corey. An older woman and full covenanted member of the Salem Village church, she also happened to publicly doubt the girls' accusations. In defending his wife, eighty-year-old Giles Corey brought the righteous wrath of the church down on his own head. Corey was a well-known and much-liked local farmer, but that didn't prevent the courts from subjecting him to a most heinous torture. But more on poor Giles Corey later. . . .

In February 1692, Capt. John Alden Jr., son of John Alden Sr. and Priscilla Mullins, original settlers of Plymouth who arrived in 1620 on the *Mayflower*, had been on his way home from Quebec after helping ransom British prisoners from Indians following the Candlemas Massacre in York (Maine). He stopped off in Salem and there was himself accused of witchcraft. He was tossed in jail, and though he thought it a foolish passing notion, his friends knew better, and fearing his bleak fate they broke him out. He later said he had to lie low in Duxbury, Massachusetts, at the home of friends until "the public had reclaimed the use of its reason."

Meanwhile, on May 10, 1692, Sarah Osborne died in jail. This was considered by the populace as a fortunate turn of events, as it lifted the onus of punishment from public shoulders.

Events spiraled so out of control that when family members objected during court proceedings, in efforts to help their loved ones on the stand, they too were arrested. Soon, accusers themselves were arrested and shared cell space with those they had accused days or weeks before. The situation in Salem and surrounding towns devolved into a free-for-all festival of suspicion, with men, women, and children pointing the finger of blame at each other. In a few instances, members of the same household hurled cries of witchery at their family members.

One woman, Mary Eastey, was arrested, only to be released again when it was found that her accusers could not confirm it was she who had afflicted them with her witchery. Though soon enough she was rearrested once her accusers were given time to reconsider.

All this happened within the first five months of 1692, and the imprisoned did not seriously consider they were going to be put to death. Up until May, the cases were of an investigative nature only. By the end of May, however, Gov. William Phips acted on the urgings of numerous counselors fearful of the growing gravity of what they considered was a rampant scourge of deviltry among them.

He convened the special Court of Oyer and Terminer to deal with the three most afflicted counties of Suffolk, Essex, and Middlesex. Prosecutions of those in jail began, and arrest warrants for thirty-six others flowed out of the courthouse doors.

By the end of May, sixty-two people were behind bars. On June 3, Bridget Bishop was put on trial before the grand jury. She was formally accused of living an amoral lifestyle, and of non-Puritan behavior—charges based largely on the fact that her clothing was black, and her coat seemed odd to the prosecutor. She was officially charged with being a witch and was hung on June 10.

The court recessed for twenty days for exploratory forays among influential churchfolk from around New England. Then it reformed with even more vigor, armed with an eight-point letter itemizing its findings composed by that expert on witchcraft, Cotton Mather. (Which begs the question, Why, if he was so knowledgeable, was he never formally accused of being a witch?) The court rolled up its collective sleeves, and prosecutions began with the speed and efficiency of a sausage factory.

So biased toward the court were elements of Mather's letter that three of the eight points rendered the others moot and virtually gave carte blanche to the court to pursue at will its desires, condemning any individuals it chose. Years later when Mather wrote about the entire episode in his book *Magnalia,* he conveniently omitted those particularly slanted and damning sections of his letter.

Arrests soon spread to other towns, and more people died in prison, awaiting trial. Then five women were hung on July 19. Another was allowed a temporary stay of execution because she was due to have a child, though she was still kept in prison. But her husband was executed on August 19. On that same day, another man, on his way to the gallows, recited the Lord's Prayer before the gathered townsfolk, something a witch was not supposed to be capable of.

He spoke so eloquently it looked as if the stunned crowd might demand he be set free. And then his accusers declared that the devil had been dictating the prayer to him. Cotton Mather came to the rescue and told the crowd that the accused was no minister and explained that the devil had a way with words. Apparently so did Mather, for shortly thereafter, the man was hung.

One month later, on September 17, 1692, eighty-year-old local farmer Giles Corey, who had been imprisoned for months for defending his equally innocent wife, Martha, was brought outside the jailhouse, his arms and legs staked out, and boards were placed over his torso. He was to be subjected to *peine forte et dure,* or pressed to death with stones, because he refused to plead guilty.

Large stones were placed on the boards. He was periodically asked if he would confess to witchcraft. Though his face purpled, his eyes bulged, and his tongue swelled out of his mouth, he refused to give the court the satisfaction of stripping him of the only things he had left: his conviction and his estate. (According to law, if a person died without admitting guilt, on his death his estate would pass to his heirs, in Corey's case, two sons-in-law.) Giles Corey lasted for two days before expiring on September 19, 1692, three days before his wife was hung.

Chief magistrate William Stoughton has bobbed in the backwash of history as one of the jerkiest judges involved in the trials. Overseeing the trials and executions in the dual roles as chief judge and prosecutor emboldened Stoughton's urge to assert Puritan primacy into the proceedings. He all but refused to accept a jury's deliberated judgment of not guilty, sending the jury back to deliberate again if its findings weren't to his liking. Unlike others he never expressed doubt, let alone regret, that acceptance of the flimsy "spectral evidence" had been a mistake in the least. His true motives, it has been surmised by historians since, were an effort to enforce unequivocal Puritan oversight throughout the region, which he felt had slipped in recent years.

Eventually the courts stopped relying solely on so-called spectral evidence, testimony given by those who claimed they were afflicted by a witch because they were able to see the apparition of their tormentor. Once this suspect method of conviction was no longer used as the sole means of determining guilt, the rate of convictions and executions dropped dramatically. Later, spectral evidence would be considered inadmissible.

Interestingly, it was Increase Mather, Cotton Mather's father, who urged the court to refrain from convicting the accused witches solely on spectral evidence. He famously wrote, "It were better that Ten Suspected Witches should escape, than that one Innocent Person should be Condemned."

In 1695, Quaker Thomas Maule, in a book critical of the poor way in which he felt the trials were handled, broadened Mather's quote, saying, "It were better that one hundred Witches should live, than that one person be put to death for a witch, which is not a Witch." This plain-spoken logic did not sit well with the still-sensitive prim powers that be, and they tossed Maule in jail for a year.

As final insult, those executed were not allowed a church burial, but were tossed ignominiously into shallow mass graves. Numerous histories tell of family members sneaking back after dark to retrieve the bodies of their dead relatives, which they reburied on their own properties.

The church magistrates even went so far as to question the four-year-old daughter of one of the accused women, taking her garbled child's answers as a confession, though the accusers thoughtfully chose to pin the rap on the tot's mother.

Sheriff George Corwin was a hypocrite and self-serving puppet of the courts before and during the time of the trials. But his comeuppance came quickly, for at the age of thirty he expired of a heart attack. A man named Phillip English, who a few years earlier had been one of the people accused of witchcraft and held by Corwin, had never been compensated for his property seized by Corwin during the trials.

English showed up at Corwin's death and demanded payment for his seized property. Until Corwin's heirs scraped up enough cash to satisfy Mr. English, the irate former accusee used Corwin's corpse as surety, not releasing it for burial until he felt adequately compensated.

And a big old heaping helping of jerkiness was clearly evident in Massachusetts governor William Phips, who had been one of the most ardent supporters of the trials. And yet, when in 1693 his own wife was suddenly accused of being a witch, Governor Phips ordered the immediate release of all prisoners still being held on charges of witchcraft. Lucky Mrs. Phips.

In the decades following the trials, various people who had been excommunicated were allowed back into the church, some posthumously. Monetary restitution also was offered, no doubt to alleviate the guilt of the accusers. Though for many it was too little too late, the sums varied from a few pounds to several hundred. The funds were distributed to those individuals who had been accused of witchcraft, or to their surviving family members.

Judge Samuel Sewall, called the "hanging judge" because of his role in the Salem Witch Trials, left a more considered legacy than most others involved. He went on to regret his role in the trials and publicly denounce them. Cold comfort to the families of the twenty innocents executed, but perhaps Sewall's public contrition—a popular Puritan pastime—helped curb future episodes of mass hysteria.

Never was a historic episode in the history of New England seemingly blessed with so many riches—a veritable Jury of Jerks, a Raft of Rascals. Men and women alike shared in the shame and humiliation that was responsible for and arose from the episode known the world over as the Salem Witch Trials.

Winnowing the number down to a manageable handful proves to be no simple matter, not solely because there were so many people caught up in the hubbub. A number of recognizable names emerge time and time again: Cotton Mather, Gov. William Phips, and Judge Samuel Sewall. And yet just as responsible for the escalating furor, and perhaps even more so, were the very friends, neighbors, and relatives of the accused women and men who paid for the unfounded and in retrospect, ludicrous crime of witchcraft.

The accusations were based on nothing more than hearsay, petty revenge, catty backbiting behavior, and childish notions spurred on and whipped into even greater waves of frenzy by religious zealots who liked to hear themselves yammer on about how the devil "hath taken possession" of Goody So-and-So. Sadly, there was little or nothing that anyone accused of witchcraft could do to refute the claims. If they said they were innocent, which they all invariably did, they were asked to prove it—something no one was able to do.

A mere child could point an accusing finger at a hardworking, tax-paying adult neighbor farmer or his wife (or both!) and quick as a snap the adults could be imprisoned, tried, charged, condemned to death, and their hard-earned lands, farms, children, possessions, and food stores were all sold, the proceeds divvied up among their friends and neighbors and relatives.

Yes, it is a difficult task to level the accusing gaze of jerkiness at a narrow few individuals responsible for stoking and feeding the fires of the witch trials, but not impossible.

The entire episode has since been labeled as an exemplary case of mass hysteria brought about by, among other lesser elements, religious extremism that birthed numerous satellite afflictions such as intolerance for any behavior not considered "godly."

And yet it was the so-called godly individuals who tormented hundreds of their fellows on nearly baseless grounds, imprisoned 150, hung nineteen people, pressed one to death, and condemned to death eight more. And of the fifty left awaiting, in cold, dank prison cells, their opportunity to plead their cases before a court already predisposed to find them guilty, at least five others died.

Accusations of witchcraft in New England had their roots in old England, but here in America, there are cases of suspected witchcraft as early as the 1630s in Boston. One poor old woman, Eunice Cole, hit the witchcraft jackpot three times during her life, surely a record. Her first offense came in 1656, while living in Boston. Though sixty-four years old at the time, she nonetheless was found guilty of being a bit witchy and received a flogging and four years in prison.

She would go on to endure several more stays in prison, including her last, which dragged on for fifteen years. When she finally expired in 1680, at age ninety, in a little hamlet in New Hampshire, villagers took no chances. They dragged her old body to a field, stabbed her through the heart with a wooden stake, and buried her in an unmarked grave.

Just after the Salem trials in 1692, a little-known follow-up series of trials took place in Stamford, Connecticut. It, too, was dominated by absurd accusations and mass paranoia.

As late as 1878, in Ipswich, Massachusetts, a follower of Christian Science accused another of her church of using "mesmeric" powers over her. Though it was eventually dismissed, it was considered the last official witchcraft trial in the United States. The trial itself was held in Salem and became known as the Second Salem Witch Trial.

## CHAPTER 10

# Jane Toppan:
# *Nurse from Hell*

How do you make a serial killer? Take one part crazy, one part neglect, one part abuse, sprinkle in alcoholism, and, for good measure, add a pinch more crazy. Then bake for a few years . . . and you have Jane Toppan, nurse and serial killer.

Between alcoholism and creeping insanity, Peter Kelley—known to his friends as "Kelley the Crack" because of his crackpot ways— had an increasingly difficult time taking care of his two youngest children after his wife, Bridget, died of consumption. So by 1863, the Kelley sisters, Delia Josephine, eight, and Honora, the younger at six, found themselves placed in the Boston Female Asylum. Their raving father begged the nuns to take them from him. Asylum officials examined the girls' clothes and general physical and mental state and determined that they were in a state of severe neglect and had probably lived through other forms of abuse as well.

It's just as well, since Peter's alcoholism and insanity grew worse as time wore on, eventually lurching completely around the bend. One story tells that while working in a tailor's shop, he tried to sew his own eyelids together and was hauled off to an institution. That sort of behavior would go a long way in explaining his daughters' later lunacy.

What must life have been like for the Kelley sisters at the Boston Female Asylum? The place was past the half-century mark at that point, established in 1799 for the purpose of housing indigent female children. The orphanage's stated mission was "to protect . . . and instruct . . . female orphans until the age of 11 years, when they are placed in respectable families."

Despite this, by November 1864, less than two years after being taken in, eight-year-old Honora became an indentured servant in the Lowell, Massachusetts, home of Mrs. Ann C. Toppan. Though Honora never really became a member of the family, she eventually assumed the surname Toppan, with "Jane" as her given name, in an effort to distance herself from her own family's seedy past. She disliked her foster mother, and though she was not abused by her foster sister, Elisabeth, young Honora/Jane grew to despise her as well.

As grim as Honora's plight seemed, her sister Delia's was even worse. She finally made it out of the orphanage in 1868, at the age of twelve, and was also placed as a servant in Athol, New York, far from her sister. Records of her life thereafter are spotty, but they indicate that Delia eventually became a prostitute and died a penniless alcoholic.

In her late teen years, Jane was courted, proposed to, and then jilted for another. No longer an indentured servant, Jane nonetheless remained at the Toppan household for another decade until her foster sister, Elisabeth, married a man named Oramel Brigham.

By 1885, twenty-eight-year-old Jane had done very well for herself. She enrolled in the nursing program at Cambridge Hospital and seemed to faculty, staff, and her fellow students to be a model nurse. But that's also when the studious, industrious Jane began to earnestly carry on her real family's line of work—madness.

An inherent curiosity would normally be encouraged in a student nurse. But Jane's wasn't the sort of experimentation praised within the confines of a laboratory. She considered the entire sick ward her lab as she began treating her patients with popular drugs of the time.

It seems the dedicated young student nurse was curious to know what those drugs, in significantly altered doses than intended, would do to her patients' nervous systems. Some might call that inspired initiative; most would consider this unlawful. But Jane did it for kicks, in what she referred to as her "scientific experiments."

She enjoyed driving the patients deep into unconsciousness and then dragging them back again from the brink of death. Her two-part chemical cocktail of choice was comprised of morphine and atropine. The latter, unlike morphine, induced more unpredictable and exciting symptoms. The effects of each canceled the other out, making the victim's death look, in all outward appearances, as if the patient had died of natural causes and not poisoning.

Jane remained unsuspected in the various deaths that occurred because she was regarded as a jovial young woman dedicated to her chosen career as a caregiver. Indeed, to her friends and coworkers, she was known as "Jolly Jane." In secret, she forged patient records and created other records out of whole cloth so that she might continue with her experiments uninterrupted.

She frequently crawled into bed with her victims, and as they were so heavily sedated, they could not cry out for help or move to fling her off them. Indeed, the only thing they could do was watch as she kissed and cradled them—and worse—shortly before she injected the second of her two-part chemical cocktail.

If one of Jane's favored patients was due to be discharged, she would falsify their records and then dose them. She would fill a new syringe with one of her cocktails to cause it to appear as if they were backsliding and needed a longer hospital stay. One of her patients during this period, Amelia Phinney, admitted years later that Jane had given her bitter-tasting pain medicine following surgery.

As the medicine took effect, Phinney recalled being startled to find that her nurse, Jolly Jane, had crawled into bed with her and began kissing her face. Luckily for the rattled patient, someone unexpectedly entered the room, preventing Jane from administering the death-dealing follow-up dose.

Mrs. Phinney awoke the next day thinking that though vivid, the experience must have been a dream. Worried that if she were wrong she might get her friendly nurse fired, the petrified patient kept this odd secret to herself until 1901, when Jane was finally arrested, long after killing numerous times.

But Jolly Jane wasn't content to merely dose the patients, lay with them, and smooch their faces. She often disrobed before climbing into bed with them, wrapping her arms around them as they breathed their last. She later said that she derived a sexual thrill at that moment when life left her unwitting charges.

She recounted years later how, one evening while working at Massachusetts General Hospital, she disrobed and climbed into bed with a female patient: "I watched in delight as she gasped her life out."

Eventually while in nursing school, Jane began to exhibit behavior that alarmed her instructors and fellow students: She developed a fondness for autopsies, attending and participating in them whenever possible.

In off-hours away from the hospital, Jane spent time working as a private nurse. To unwind, she visited local watering holes, tippling with as much gusto as had her alcoholic father and sister, and descending into dark moods that contrasted with her daytime persona. Jane was busy not only in the hospital, but outside it as well. In 1895 and 1897, she murdered her married landlords, Israel and Lovey Dunham.

Despite the increased mortality rates and her proclivity for dallying with the dead, Jane completed the nursing program in 1887. She was eventually discharged from her trainee position at Massachusetts General Hospital because she left the ward without permission one day, a big no-no. Ironically this meant she would not receive her official nursing license, though her diploma had been signed and her final examinations had been passed.

Remarkably, she was merely fired from one hospital job when a number of her patients were found dead of medicinal overdoses. Likewise she was compelled to leave her next place of employment in Cambridge for overprescribing drugs.

In 1899, while vacationing at Cape Cod with her foster sister, Elisabeth, now married to Oramel Brigham, Jane brought her dark skills into the family circle: She slowly poisoned Elisabeth, keeping her lingering for days before finally finishing her off.

And after Elisabeth finally succumbed to death, Jane told the shocked and grieving Oramel that her sister had wanted her to have her gold watch and chain. Oramel agreed, knowing this sort

JANE
TOPPAN

*Nurse "Jolly" Jane Toppan got her kicks by injecting patients with a lethal cocktail, then cuddling naked with them as they died.*

of generous gift would be in keeping with his wife's demeanor. What he didn't know is that Jane later pawned the keepsakes.

But it didn't end there. Crazy Nurse Jane visited her brother-in-law frequently. And coincident with two such visits, in subsequent years, Oramel's housekeeper, Miss Florence Calkins, became ill and died, in January 1900, smack dab during one of Jane's visits. And the very next year, also during one of Jane's annual visits, another houseguest, Oramel's sister, Mrs. Edna Bannister, of Tunbridge, Vermont, came down with a sudden illness and died the following day, as luck would have it, right in Jane's arms.

A bit late, Oramel began to suspect something was not right, but before he could do anything about it, he also mysteriously came down with a strange illness. Everyone agreed it was a good thing dear Jane was there to nurse the poor man. Oramel lingered at death's door for days before rebounding with surprising vigor, only to be laid low again the next day. This roller-coaster ride was due solely to Jane's injections.

This went on for some time, until finally Jane let the poor man recover—not an outcome many of her patients were allowed. She had hoped to prove to him that she alone was able to provide comfort to him, for she was in love with him. Their on-again, off-again dating ended there. The haggard Oramel tossed her out on her ear.

While working as a private nurse in Cambridge and Boston, she had rented a cottage in Cataumet, on Cape Cod, from a family named Davis. The rental would prove to be her undoing because, over the course of the summer of 1901, Nurse Jane went on a bit of a spree and murdered the entire Davis family.

Jane had neglected to pay rent for a number of months, and it was decided that Mary Davis, the wife of the home's owner, Alden Davis, would be sent to Cambridge to talk with Nurse Jane, whom they all liked exceedingly well. They thought that they might somehow help her, for certainly such a popular private nurse shouldn't have money troubles.

Mary Davis visited Jane and ended up returning home to Cataumet in a coffin. Mary had been accompanied on the short trip by her daughter Genevieve, who surmised that perhaps it had been the summer heat that had gotten to her dear old mother. She asked Jane to return with them to the Cape for the funeral. Jane agreed and stayed with the family. Within days, Genevieve was found dead in her bed. She had been depressed, after all, since her mother died. Perhaps she had killed herself? Rumors flew, but one thing was agreed upon—it was a blessing that dear nurse Jane Toppan was there for them all. Such a rock. Such a giving soul.

And then, oddly enough, within days old Alden, too, gave up the ghost. And who could blame him? His wife and daughter, after all, had just died. The only people left in the household were Jane Toppan and Maryanne Gibbs, the married daughter of Alden and Mary and sister of Genevieve, all so recently deceased. And within a week, so was Maryanne.

Her husband, Irving Gibbs, was a ship's captain. And when Captain Gibbs received word that his wife had also just died of natural causes, he became incensed, as he knew his wife had been hale and hearty. Yet doctors could find no trace of poison or foul play.

But what the now-dead Davis family didn't know was that, months before, Jolly Jane had fallen under suspicion for poisoning a patient in Lowell, Massachusetts. In fact, she was being quietly—and too slowly—investigated by the district attorney's office in Middlesex County. When the DA learned of the mass demise of the Davis family, he requested that the bodies of the two Davis sisters, Genevieve and Maryanne, be exhumed.

It didn't take long for the authorities to issue a warrant for Nurse Jane. She was tracked down and arrested on October 29, 1901, in Amherst, New Hampshire.

Before she went to trial, Jane confessed to killing the Davis family and explained how she went about it—by alternating her trademark tinctures of atropine and morphine. A number of medical professionals listened to and examined Jane and came to the conclusion with the court that Jane was indeed clinically and certifiably insane, and that it was probably a hereditary condition, given that her father, the eyelid-sewing madman, and her sister had both ended up in asylums.

During her trial, which began in 1902, she confessed to killing eleven people, and claimed her intention had been "to have killed more people—helpless people—than any man or woman who ever lived." She had kept up her dark dalliances with the dying for years and claimed she was dispensing not death but "mercy," and she referred to herself as the "Angel of Death."

Jane was found not guilty by reason of insanity, and sentenced to life imprisonment at the State Lunatic Hospital at Taunton. After the trial she confessed to her attorney that she had actually killed thirty-one people in all, strong supporting evidence of which could be found for twenty of the unfortunates; the remaining eleven remained suspected. Jane never expressed remorse but did seem surprised at her propensity for not feeling anything remotely like remorse.

After she was committed to the asylum, she said, "I might say I feel hilarious, but perhaps that expresses it too strongly. I do not know the feeling of fear and I do not know the feeling of remorse, although I understand perfectly what these words mean. . . . Why don't I feel sorry and grieve over it? I don't know. I seem to have a sort of paralysis of thought and reason."

Honora Kelley/Jane Toppan lived for another thirty-six years at the State Lunatic Hospital at Taunton, reaching the ripe old age of eighty-one before dying on August 17, 1938. Early in her stay, she refused to eat, convinced that she was being poisoned by the staff. Eventually she resumed eating, her appetite for killing having been supplanted by her appetite for food.

Over the years Jane's mental state dissipated further until she seemed nothing more than a harmless old woman. Though even as an inmate in the asylum, she frequently tried to lure staff nurses to procure morphine so they might roam the ward together, promising them, "We will have a lot of fun watching them die." Jolly Jane to the end.

Jane Toppan wasn't Massachusetts's first murderer, nor sadly will she be the last. But who was the first convicted murderer in the New World? That would be one John Billington, one of the original Pilgrims—not for religious reasons, though. He, along with his wife and two sons, chose to head to the New World to outrun John's mounting pile of debt. Billington wasn't one of the sharper knives in the drawer of humanity, and it seems that his offspring inherited the family dimwit gene.

They'd barely anchored the *Mayflower* when one of his sons thought it might be all sorts of fun to fire one of his dad's pistols belowdecks—not far from an open barrel of gunpowder. Billington the younger nearly succeeded in blowing apart the ship, and all of the New World's founding Pilgrims with it.

On shore, Billington tried to weasel out of the mandatory service the colonists required of all able men. They threatened to hogtie him, but he whined, and they relented. Not surprisingly they regretted this, as he proved to be a lazy man and a lousy worker.

Soon Billington became part of a small group of men plotting to overthrow the Puritan leaders of the fledgling colony. When buttonholed, he denied his involvement in the plot. But a close eye was kept on the weasel. In the following decade, Billington continued to rant and rave about the strict policies of Gov. William Bradford. He was tolerated, barely, and considered a "knave" by many.

In 1630 Billington got into an argument with another man, John Newcomen, and shot at him with his musket. But being a poor shot, Billington merely gave the man a nonfatal wound to the shoulder. Soon after, however, Newcomen came down with a cold, grew weak, and infection in the wound turned gangrenous. Within days, Newcomen was dead.

Governor Bradford, long weary of John Billington, about whom he had referred uncharitably in a letter to a church deacon years before ("a knave, and so will live and die"), had Billington arrested and then tried, with the result that Billington was found guilty of the crime of murder. This made John Billington America's premier convicted murderer, and his victim, the first recorded homicide in this brave new land. Billington was hung on September 30, 1630. His sons, however, propagated. Oh dear. . . .

And of course, the mention of murder in Massachusetts, and in New England, should not come to pass without special note of one Lizzy Borden, perhaps the most notorious female killer in the history of the United States. Even more so because she was accused and then acquitted of the horrific crimes of patricide and (step-) matricide on August 4, 1892—with an axe! Crimes that most people—and ample evidence—agree she did indeed commit.

She was acquitted of the crimes despite the fact that prior to that she had purchased prussic acid at a local hardware store, allegedly to clean her sealskin coat, and her family had come down with an illness, the symptoms of which could be attributed to such poisoning. Despite the fact that the police tripped her up in repeated lies about the crimes, despite the fact that she had ample motive (her father was a wealthy, tight-fisted man, and she did not want to share an inheritance with her stepsiblings), despite the fact that after the murders she was caught stuffing a dress with dark stains on it into the cook stove in the kitchen, despite a dizzying number of other impressive and seemingly damning pieces of evidence, Lizzy Borden was acquitted, enjoyed her sizable inheritance, and lived to the age of sixty-six, dying in 1927 of pneumonia.

Despite the fact that Borden's stepmother received nineteen axe strokes and her father eleven, a rhyme made up at the time for children to skip rope to, and still fondly recalled by many today, states:

*Lizzie Borden took an axe*
*And gave her mother forty whacks.*
*When she saw what she had done*
*She gave her father forty-one.*

## CHAPTER 11

# New World Slavers:
# *Kidnappers for Fun and Profit*

E nglish explorer, kidnapper, and slaver George Weymouth gained notoriety as captain of a 1605 expedition reconnoitering the coast of what is now the state of Maine. He acted on behalf of the nobleman, Sir Ferdinando Gorges, governor of Plymouth, England, who, being wealthy and desirous of seeing his name on a map, wished to stake a claim in the New World. The efforts (by way of much funding) Gorges expended led him to be called the father of English colonization in North America, though oddly enough, he never once visited his beloved New World.

He was so successful in this undertaking that he founded the province of Maine, on August 10, 1622, though he named it New Somersetshire, which then included portions of what we now call Maine, New Hampshire, Vermont, Quebec, and New Brunswick. Alas, Gorges died penniless in 1647, having blown through a vast fortune underwriting forays to the New World. His heir, a grandson also named Ferdinando, sold his family's last ragged land claims to the commonwealth of Massachusetts in 1677 for 1,250 pounds.

But back in 1605, Gorges bankrolled the Weymouth expedition, and on March 5 of that year, Weymouth captained the ship *Archangel* out of English waters. He and his crew sailed westward across the Atlantic, eventually spying land more than two months later. On May 17, 1605, Weymouth joined his initial exploratory crew aboard a lifeboat that landed on the shore of Monhegan, a robust, thousand-acre island twelve miles off what is now mid-coast Maine. Today it is most famous as an artist's colony, but back then the island was only inhabited seasonally by the local Patuxet Indians, who used it as a fishing base.

Weymouth and his men were not the first European explorers to set foot on Monhegan, however. Bartholomew Gosnold, an Englishman, sailed there in 1602; Martin Pring, another Englishman, touched toe to shore in 1603; and famed French explorer Samuel de Champlain made a pit stop there in 1604. It became a fishing camp for the British, too, even before the Plymouth Colony was settled—the grounds around Monhegan offered riches in cod, which was dried and then shipped to Europe. It also didn't hurt that the local Indians were willing to trade their luxurious, hard-earned furs for cheap baubles.

But all this lay a few years in the future. When George Weymouth and his men landed on Monhegan, they were acting on behalf of their sponsor, Gorges, seeking ideal locations to establish colonists. Though the Algonquin called the place Monchiggon, in their lingo meaning "out-to-sea island," Weymouth, in typical bold-explorer fashion, called it Saint George, in honor of England's patron saint (or himself).

Accompanying Weymouth on the expedition was a chap named James Rosier. Son of a clergyman, he had visited there three years earlier with the Gosnold expedition. On Weymouth's trip, Rosier recorded his detailed accounts of the Weymouth expedition that were later published, posthumously, under the windy title of *A true relation of the most prosperous voyage made this present yeere 1605, by Captaine George Weymouth, in the discovery of the North Part of Virginia.*

Rosier's initial impressions of Monhegan were evocative and alluring and helped contribute to later colonization: "This lland is woody, growen with Firre, Birch, Oke and Beech, as farre as we say along the shore; and so likely to be within. On the verge grow Gooseberries, Strawberries, Wild pease, and Wilde rose bushes." The ship roved the island, marveling at the great quantity and variety of natural resources, noting numerous fruits, tree species, and that the shore fishing was excellent for them. No word on whether they were under orders to procure local folk for English amusement back home.

On May 30, back on board their anchored ship, the English sailors got their first glimpse of the natives. Rosier wrote:

*This day, about five a clocke in the afternoone, we in the shippe espied three Canoas comming towards vs, which went to the iland adjoining, where they went a shore, and very quickly had made a fire, about which they stood beholding our ship: to whom we made signes with our hands and hats, weffing vnto them to come vnto vs, because we had not seene any of the people yet. They sent one Canoa with three men, one of which, when they came neere vnto vs, spake in his language very lowd and very boldly: seeming as though he would know why we were there, and by pointing with his oare towards the sea, we conjectured he ment we should be gone. But when we shewed them kniues and their vse, by cutting of stickes and other trifles, as combs and glasses, they came close aboard our ship, as desirous to entertaine our friendship. To these we gaue such things as we perceiued they liked, when wee shewed them the vse: bracelets, rings, peacocke feathers, which they stucke in their haire, and Tabacco pipes. After their departure to their company on the shore, presently came foure other in another Canoa: to whom we gaue as to the former, vsing them with as much kindnes as we could.*

*The shape of their body is very proportionable, they are wel countenanced, not very tal nor big, but in stature like to vs: they paint their bodies with blacke, their faces, some with red, some with blacke, and some with blew.*

*Their clothing is Beauers skins, or Deares skins, cast ouer them like a mantle, and hanging downe to their knees, made fast together vpon the shoulder with leather; some of them had sleeues, most had none; some had buskins of such leather tewed: they haue besides a peece of Beauers skin betweene their legs, made fast about their waste, to couer their priuities.*

*They suffer no haire to grow on their faces, but on their head very long and very blacke, which those that haue wiues, binde vp behinde with a leather string, in a long round knot.*

*They seemed all very ciuill and merrie: shewing tokens of much thankefulnesse, for those things we gaue them. We found them then (as after) a people of exceeding good inuention, quicke vnderstanding and readie capacitie.*

*Their Canoas are made without any iron, of the bark of a birch tree, strengthened within with ribs and hoops of wood, in so good fashion, with such excellent ingenious art, as they are able to beare seuen or eight persons, far exceeding any in the Indies.*

*One of their Canoas came not to vs, wherein we imagined their women were: of whom they are (as all Saluages) very jealous.*

*When I signed unto them they should goe sleepe, because it was night, they vnderstood presently, and pointed that at the shore, right against our ship, they would stay all night: as they did.*

*The next morning very early, came one Canoa abord vs againe with three Saluages, whom we easily then enticed into our ship, and vnder the decke: where we gaue them porke, fish, bred and pease, all which they did eat; and this I noted, they would eat nothing raw, either fish or flesh. They maruelled much and much looked vpon the making of our canne and kettle, so they did at a head-peece and at our guns, of which they are most fearefull, and would fall flat downe at the report of them. At their departure I signed vnto them, that if they would bring me such skins as they ware I would giue them kniues, and such things as I saw they most liked, which the chiefe of them promised to do by that time the Sunne should be beyond the middest of the firmament; this I did to bring them to an vnderstanding of exchange, and that they might conceiue the intent of our comming to them to be for no other end.*

*About 10 a clocke this day we descried our Shallop
returning toward vs, which so soone as we espied, we certainly conjectured our Captaine had found some vnex-
pected harbour, further vp towards the maine to bring the
ship into, or some riuer; knowing his determination and
resolution, not so suddenly else to make return: which
when they came neerer they expressed by shooting volleies
of shot; and when they were come within Musket shot, they
gaue vs a volley and haled vs, then we in the shippe gaue
them a great peece and haled them.*

*Thus we welcomed them; who gladded vs exceedingly
with their joifull relation of their happie discouerie, which
shall appeare in the sequele. And we likewise gaue them
cause of mutuall joy with vs, in discoursing of the kinde
ciuility we found in a people, where we little expected any
sparke of humanity.*

It is curious, then, that though these English explorers were
quite obviously impressed with the Indians, as evinced by Rosier's
revealing accounts, that the captain should consider enslaving
some of them, with no apparent regard for the intended victims
or their families. But Weymouth did finally settle on the notion
of kidnapping several of them. Near the mouth of the Pemaquid
River, on June 4, 1605, suspicious that the Indians might be plotting against them (I wonder why they'd think that), Weymouth
and his gang determined to capture some of the "savages": "We
determined so soone as we could to take some of them, least (being
suspicious we had discovered their plots) they should absent
themselves from us."

Under the pretense of inviting the "savages" on board his ship
for a grand meal, Weymouth and his men managed to inveigle
only three takers. He plied them with alcohol, and soon the addled
natives were imprisoned belowdecks. Then he and his men loaded
up a dinghy with baubles and trinkets for trading, and ashore they
attempted to lure more Indians to the ship with promise of greater

treasure. The Indians sensed something was amiss, so rather than lose out on the situation, Weymouth ordered his men to seize two more male Indians. They manhandled them, dragging them by the hair on their heads, though the Indians gave them a tough time of it. They also managed to steal two birch-bark canoes as extra loot. Here is Rosier's account of the incident:

> *We vsed little delay, but suddenly laid hands vpon them. And it was as much as fiue or sixe of vs could doe to get them into the light horseman. For they were strong and so naked as our best hold was by their long haire on their heads; and we would haue beene very loath to haue done them any hurt, which of necessity we had beene constrained to haue done if we had attempted them in a multitude, which we must and would, rather than haue wanted them, being a matter of great importance for the full accomplement of our voyage. Thus we shipped fiue Saluages, two Canoas, with all their bowes and arrows.*

Two days later, on June 6, as Weymouth traveled southward, two canoes with more Indians paddled up to the *Archangel* and tried to coax Weymouth and his men to come ashore to trade. But Weymouth, now skittish and suspicious of the natives' motives, wanted neither to entertain them aboard nor to go ashore with them, fearful that these newcomers would discover the other Indians he had locked belowdecks as prisoners.

The Patuxet Indians Weymouth captured were named Manida, Skettawarroes, Dehanada, Assacumet, and Tisquantum. The latter, who came to be known as Squanto, went on to prove indispensible some years later to the survival of the first Pilgrim settlers in the New World. But before he could do so, he would go on a long journey far from his home.

In July, after taking much from the land and the sea, including five prisoners and their canoes and other accoutrements, Weymouth's expedition sailed for Europe. Three of the Patuxet were given as gifts to the expedition's sponsor, Sir Ferdinando Gorges. They were taught English and the next year, two of them, Assacumet and Manida, were sent on another Gorges expedition to the West Indies and Puerto Rico, under Capt. Henry Challoung.

Sir John Popham received the other two enslaved Indians. The hubbub caused among Londoners on seeing these "savages" is said to have inspired William Shakespeare to write a line in his play *The Tempest:* "Any strange beast there makes a man / when they will not give a doit to relieve a lame beggar, they will lay out ten to see a dead Indian."

In England, Weymouth had the distinction of having a North American tree species, *Pinus strobus,* or eastern white pine, named after him. One wonders how the "Weymouth pine" feels about the dubious honor.

And what of James Rosier, diligent scribe and conspirator to that early and fateful kidnapping during George Weymouth's 1605 trip to the New World? In 1608 he traveled to Rome and enrolled in the Jesuit English College. Oddly enough, in explaining his virtues upon his arrival, he conveniently omitted his 1605 voyage to the New World with Weymouth. Could it be that he looked back on the filching of men as vaguely un-Christian behavior? Rosier was ordained as a Jesuit in 1609, but he died later that year while traveling back to England.

Many history books relate how the Indians were well treated, educated, showered with lavish gifts and praise, and then returned safely to their families' waiting arms. Not exactly. . . .

An expedition in 1611 to Maine and Massachusetts waters proved, from a slaver's point of view, to be a bountiful trek. By the time Capt. Edward Harlow's ship made it to an island (now Martha's Vineyard) off Cape Cod, he had already been to Maine waters and had captured three Indians from Monhegan Island: Pechmo, Monopet, and Pekenimne.

Pechmo revealed himself to be wilier than his fellows and at the first opportunity jumped ship, stole a dinghy tied to the ship's side, then fled to shore. Undaunted, Captain Harlow headed to what is now Nantucket, where he captured Sakaweston, who would spend many years in England, and then fight on her behalf in Bohemia in the 1620s. Shortly thereafter he dropped anchor off Cape Cod and kidnapped Epenow and Coneconam. By the time Harlow set sail for England, he had kidnapped twenty-nine Native American slaves.

A Gorges-funded expedition in 1606 did not go as planned. The ship was captured by the Spanish and taken to Spain, where the crew, including the enslaved Indians, was imprisoned in Seville. Eventually, the Indian Assacumet, as a "savage," was deemed of lesser value than his fellow captives and was sent to Gorges's home in England. There he shared accommodations with Epenow, one of the Wampanoags captured in the 1611 expedition and who had subsequently been displayed in London to the delight of the citified crowds.

In 1614, Assacumet, with Epenow, again ventured forth on a Gorges expedition to the New World, this time to present-day Martha's Vineyard. The reason for this latest expedition was the greed of Epenow's master, Sir Gorges himself. Epenow hauled out a map and pinpointed a spot, now Martha's Vineyard, and told Gorges that the spot was filthy rich in gold. It didn't take much convincing for Gorges to fund a new expedition, this time captained by Nicholas Hobson, with Epenow acting as guide and translator. They arrived and were greeted by canoes full of gracious Wampanoags. Epenow secretly discussed plans for escape with his tribesmen, some of whom were his relatives.

By the following day, however, Hobson had become suspicious of Epenow's motives. He made the Indian wear long clothes that his men could grasp easily should the Indian decide to flee. He once again invited the Wampanoag aboard his ship, but they insisted Epenow come to the rail to translate. He began to do so and then leapt overboard. At the same time, Hobson's men grabbed his flowing garments and managed to gain a handful—but Epenow was too powerful, and the Wampanoag loosed volley after volley of arrows at the ship. Though both sides suffered loss of life, Epenow

*Long before the Pilgrims broke bread with Indians, white European explorers kidnapped boatloads of natives and sold them as slaves in Spain.*

LIBRARY OF CONGRESS

had gained his freedom, and Hobson departed without an ounce of gold and minus one enslaved Indian.

Epenow went on to become a sachem, or leader, of his people, and when the first wave of Pilgrims arrived at Plymouth six years later, he led a group of resistance fighters against them, convinced they were there to steal his people.

Meanwhile, back in Old Blighty, Tisquantum (Squanto), as a captive in England, learned English and became an indispensible member of various Gorges's funded expeditions to the New World. His chief function as an interpreter was most useful to the English expeditions. In 1614, once again en route to visit his people, the Patuxet, Squanto was one of a number of Indians captured by Englishman Thomas Hunt, lieutenant under explorer John Smith.

Hunt was an unsavory sort and headed for Malaga, Spain, with his boatload of ill-gotten goods. He intended to sell the kidnapped Indians, as well as stolen foods, fish, game, and furs, for a tidy personal profit. When a group of Spanish friars learned of Hunt's intentions, they made off with the unsold slaves and worked to convert the "savages" to Christianity.

Squanto proved an apt pupil, as he already had ample knowledge of the language and of many whites' customs. He ended up in London, working for a shipbuilder named John Slany for a few years. He tried several times to get back to North America before finally doing so in 1619, aboard an exploratory ship helmed by John Smith, captain of his former kidnapper.

When Squanto landed, he found out that most of his people and those of another close tribe, the Wampanoag, were all but wiped out the previous year by an epidemic that historians believe was probably smallpox brought to the New World by the Europeans. Squanto had developed an immunity to the disease from time spent among the English.

His greatest contributions to history were yet to come, though. He helped the inexperienced, naïve Pilgrims survive early years of starvation and privation. Without his early assistance and generous sharing of gardening, hunting, and fishing skills, it is probable that the Pilgrims would not have survived in their strange, new homeland.

In the coming two years, Squanto's assistance to the new settlers' leaders would prove indispensible. Not only was he an apt translator, but he helped broker a long-standing peace between the new arrivals and the local tribes of Indians. He became a valued and trusted member of the Pilgrims' community at Plymouth.

In 1622, while returning from a meeting helping to bolster peace between the Wampanoag and the Pilgrims, Squanto became ill, bleeding from the nose. He died several days later. It was suspected that he had been poisoned by the Wampanoag for an earlier perceived affront to the sachem. Despite this, a fifty-year peace continued between the Wampanoag and the Pilgrims.

Nonetheless, incidents of kidnapping and enslaving Native Americans would continue for hundreds of years in various ways with the coming colonization of the New World. Man's inherent urge for profit and power would lead the societally dominant white Europeans to enslave not only Native Americans but to cast their net further and import Africans to sell as commodities in a trade that would last hundreds of years. Even when they were well intentioned, the whites managed to subject Native Americans to harm on a number of occasions.

The smallpox epidemic that had ravaged Squanto's people had been unwittingly brought to the New World in 1617 by English and Dutch fishermen. Ninety percent of the native population along Massachusetts Bay were killed by the deadly virus.

Smallpox would be used intentionally little more than a century later by British North America governor-general Jeffery Amherst (namesake of the Massachusetts town and college) in the first attempted use in North America of biological warfare.

In 1763, during hostilities between the British and Native Americans on the frontier (what is now Pennsylvania) following the French and Indian War, Governor-General Amherst approved a plan to distribute smallpox-infected blankets in an attempt at all-out genocide of the Indians.

He also vowed to support any other such methods that might, in his words, "serve to Extirpate this Execrable Race." What a jerk.

## CHAPTER 12

# Neal S. Dow:
## *The Napoleon of Temperance*

Zealots of any stripe conflict with the very reason for the founding of this country—or at least the ideal we've all come to embrace: tolerance of each other's individual freedoms. The notion that an individual or a group knows what's best for others is odious to most Americans, who by nature are a fairly independent lot. So when extremists sink their teeth into a personal cause, even one that might well result in benefitting everyone, fur flies and lines are drawn in the sand. Such was the case with Neal Dow and, to a larger extent, his beloved temperance movement, the long-term societal effects of which are still felt with a shiver every time the word *prohibition* is uttered.

Neal Dow, also known as the Napoleon of Temperance and the Father of Prohibition, can hardly be faulted for his lifelong dedication to civic mindedness and service to the public good. He has, however, earned his inclusion here not because he was a teetotaler, but because he was a teetotaler who forced his own brand of sobriety on Maine. As mayor of Portland in 1855, he illegally stored a large quantity of rum at city hall (he said it was purely for medicinal purposes). When this supply was discovered, a parched crowd of two thousand Portlanders rallied and railed. Dow, worried that the rowdy mob might grow even rowdier, ordered in the militia. The result? One man was killed and seven were wounded in what became known as the Portland Rum Riot.

He was tried, though acquitted, of violating the very law he helped put in place—prohibition. But the incident marred his campaign for the governor's seat.

It will come as little surprise, then, to learn that Dow was born, on March 20, 1804, into a devout Portland, Maine, Quaker

*Neal S. Dow's lifelong quest to inflict his teetotaling ways on all of America overshadowed his many admirable traits.*

LIBRARY OF CONGRESS

family whose teachings fervently eschewed the consumption of alcohol. It has also been said that during Dow's formative years, down by the waterfront at Portland, he was forced by drunks to engage in fisticuffs . . . with a monkey. That would pretty much put anyone off booze.

Denied the opportunity to study at college, largely due to his strict father's beliefs that such institutions would only foster illicit behavior, young Neal instead entered into his father's tannery business and eventually became a partner before taking over and expanding it into a much larger and more successful venture. But he had a yearning to participate in society. He also rose above the education denied him by scrimping, saving, and buying books whenever he could. Looking back from his later years, Dow reckoned that for the times, he had developed the largest private library in the state of Maine.

He went on to form the Young Men's Abstinence Society and was keen on taking the movement to an ever-larger audience. While still a young man himself, Dow exhibited a keen intellect and facility for extolling the virtues of sobriety, no mean feat in a state such as Maine, where the consumption of alcohol per person was three times greater than it is today.

Dow would later write in his autobiography, "It was the rule to quit work at eleven in the morning and again at four in the afternoon to drink. . . . Many grocers kept rum in a tub right outside on the sidewalk, just as lemonade is seen today on the fourth of July."

He became a bright light and favorite speaker in the Maine Temperance Union, a local affiliate of the national movement.

As a young man, instead of joining the militia, as required of all men his age, Dow joined the volunteer fire department, confident that there would be less drinking and debauchery taking place. It turns out to have been a good fit for the young man, as he was able to impose his growing formidable will on the powers that be in the department to such an extent that he convinced them to hold the annual fire department's celebration sans alcohol, an unheard-of accomplishment for the times. This coup, in turn, produced impressive statewide notice for him that he parlayed into PR for his budding political aspirations, which culminated in a successful run for the office of mayor in his hometown of Portland.

In 1838 he helped found the Maine Temperance Union when a small but devout group split from the Maine Temperance Society in a disagreement over whether wine should be exempted from their preachings. The new organization—and so, Dow—frowned on the taking of wine, seeing it as demonic as all other forms of alcohol.

Dow was also an avid and outspoken abolitionist, as were many of his fellow temperance union members, so it was natural to combine promotion of outright bans of liquor and slavery. In 1849 he helped draw up a law purportedly banning the sale of liquor. Although it was weak-kneed from the start, poorly worded and fuzzy in its enforcement and application, the attempt did help Dow wedge a boot in the door and served to fire up Dow's zeal to greater heights.

He worked for the next several years to get his own more meticulously worded antiliquor measure enacted. And in 1851, when Dow was first elected mayor of Portland as a Temperance Whig, he promptly set about using this new position to influence the legislature and governor to enact his tough temperance law. On June 2, 1851, it passed, though not without much opposition. Nonetheless this statewide stricture propelled Dow to national fame as a temperance man to be reckoned with.

Dow's pet project, known as the Maine Law, had a number of effects locally and nationally. He was a very unpopular man in Portland, the city of which he was mayor and which he had all but wrung out of alcohol. He used it as a test case for what he was convinced would be the thorough effectiveness of his law. But the large population of Irish laborers in that city was unimpressed. They wanted the right to tipple at will after—and frequently during—a long day at work. But the law was the law, and Dow informed the police to tolerate no challenge to it.

Dow was also becoming a popular lecturer in ever-widening circles and traveled throughout the Northeast and beyond, railing against the evils of slavery and booze. At the same time, those opposing his law became more unified, concentrated, and vocal in their efforts at opposing it. Despite this growing anti-antimovement, Neal Dow was again elected mayor of Portland in 1855.

During his mayoral tenure, he had stored a large quantity of rum at city hall, which he claimed was purely for medicinal and mechanical purposes. His Maine Law of 1851 allowed for the manufacture and sale of such alcohol, though not for any other purpose. As mayor of Portland, he was doing as he ought—the $1,600 worth of alcohol he had stored in city vaults was meant solely for distribution to doctors and pharmacists.

Anyone remotely familiar with Neal Dow and his lifelong crusade against the consumption of demon alcohol would have a tough time believing his detractors, who claimed Dow had reserved the booze for his own private use. If so, it would certainly be well aged, for a drop would never touch his lips. Dow didn't help his own argument, though, as the city aldermen took him to task—and later, to court—for failing to get their permission for the purchase, a requisite component of his own law that the stickler Dow failed to follow.

When news of this supply was leaked, the public grew infuriated, either being truly ignorant of the purpose for which the alcohol was reserved, or choosing to ignore it and venting their anger at the one man who had singlehandedly taken from them something many of them very much enjoyed—and even identified with on a cultural level. Alcohol was especially important to the local Irish immigrant community, with whom Dow had butted heads and locked horns countless times over the years.

Now they were handed an excuse to allow their rage to overrun reason. On the afternoon of June 2, 1855, a crowd of several hundred parched Portlanders had gathered outside city hall, hurling cries of "Hypocrite!" at their reviled mayor. As the day progressed, the crowd swelled in size, of anywhere from one thousand to three thousand (a significant number considering Portland's entire population was roughly twenty thousand), rallying and railing outside city hall.

The people's anger grew to dangerous levels when they realized that the police refused to hand over the liquor supply. The crowd's violent demeanor escalated beyond name-calling to pushing, shoving, and rock throwing. Soon, fistfights broke out among the protestors. The police, aware that the crowd was about to exceed the ability to contain them, requested that the mayor call in the militia, and Dow readily complied.

When the crowd refused to break up after the militia ordered it to do so, Dow committed what many look back on as the biggest mistake of his public life. He ordered the militia to open fire on the crowd. The result? One man, a sailor from Deer Isle named John

Robbins, was killed, and seven were wounded. This took the starch out of the crowd's zeal, but that dark event, known as the Portland Rum Riot, cast a well-earned pall over Dow's later political career.

He received wide and long criticism for what many of his friends and many more of his detractors considered his heavy-handed handling of the incident. The Portland Rum Riot would mar his campaign for the governor's seat and cling to his political life like a bad odor for the rest of his days.

Ironically Dow was later put on trial for violating the very law he helped put in place. It seems he had acquired the "medicinal and mechanical" alcohol improperly. One would think that the very architect of the law would take special pains to ensure all his i's were dotted and t's crossed. It was, after all, a law he defended with a fierceness that left teetotalers quaking in his wake. He was acquitted, but the trial and the Portland Rum Riot were primary reasons the law was repealed the following year.

Still it didn't do much to slow the man down. In 1857, Dow traveled to England on the first of three such trips, lecturing against those topics he considered most evil. Despite the fact that he was brought up a nonwarring Quaker, so fervently did Dow believe in the abolishment of slavery that he volunteered for service in the Civil War at age fifty-seven. Indeed he was no stranger to the cause: His home was a secret stop on the Underground Railroad. Dow saw slavery and alcohol as inextricably linked—and they were. The rum trade was largely funded by the importation of slaves from West Africa and the West Indies. Dow fervently believed that if one could be stopped, the other would be as well.

On November 23, 1861, he was made a colonel of the 13th Maine Infantry. He saw much active duty and helped in the capture of New Orleans. In part due to his actions there, he was promoted to the position of brigadier general in April 1862 and commanded the captured Confederate Forts Jackson and St. Philip, as well as the district of Florida.

At the siege of Port Hudson in Louisiana on May 27, 1863, Dow sustained wounds in his right arm and left thigh. While he was convalescing, he was captured by enemy forces. He spent the next eight months as a prisoner in Richmond and then Mobile before being part of a prisoner exchange that included swapping him for Gen. Robert E. Lee's son, Gen. William Henry Fitzhugh Lee. By then it was late February 1864. He held on until November of that year and then resigned his post in the army as the result of poor health.

Once home in Maine, it didn't take Dow long to regain his health enough to wade back into politics and take up his accustomed positions on hot-button topics, most notably his old favorite, temperance. In 1865 he cofounded the National Temperance Society and Publishing House. The society would be a vocal presence and advocate for national temperance for decades to come, publishing one billion pages of temperance material and propaganda in its first half century.

Though a lifelong Republican, a trait shared by most Prohibitionists, the years after the war saw a shift in politics and support for such parties. The Brewers Association of the United States became a major supporter of the Republican Party, an unconscionable development for Dow and other prohibitionists. In reaction, they formed the Prohibition Party in 1869.

In 1880, Dow was nominated as the Prohibition Party's candidate for the office of president of the United States. He came in fourth, however, receiving only 10,305 votes.

As an old man near the end of his days, Dow wrote his autobiography, *The Reminiscences of Neal Dow, Recollections of Eighty Years.* Ever temperate-minded, he hoped "that a simply told story of the temperance movement in Maine may stimulate some who fear God and love their fellow-men to aid in securing the protection of society from the infinite evils resulting from the liquor-traffic."

On his ninetieth birthday, when congratulated on reaching that milestone, he said, "All this is nothing to me so long as a liquor-saloon exists under the sanction of law, or with the consent of officials in violation of law. This celebration of my birthday is gratifying to me, chiefly as testimony of the widespread appreciation of the magnitude of the evil I have antagonized, and as an assurance that, although my personal efforts must soon cease forever, the object for which I have labored will in time be secured."

Well, not quite, Mr. Dow. Nowadays, liquor sales are a major source of revenue for the state and country he so unflinchingly served and for which he worked so diligently. And while we can and should be grateful for his selfless efforts for society on a local and national level, there is much to be praised for moderation, lest the screaming and zealous behavior of the squelcher become a mania that spreads far and wide. "Balance in all things, moderation in all things," as someone once said.

Neal S. Dow's legacy would be felt for decades after his death at the age of ninety-three on October 2, 1897. Indeed his mighty influence can still be felt throughout the nation and the world, as temperance leagues still exist and attitudes toward moderation continue to thrive in pockets. The national ban on alcohol and the Prohibition movement of 1920 through 1933 are the most lasting reminders of the pros and cons of temperance.

And on a less publicly antagonistic level, Dow was the father of Fred Dow, a powerful figure on the Maine political scene for years. Fred was the first Republican speaker of the house and founded the Portland Club (still in existence), which at the time required that its members be teetotaling male Republicans. Today, the Portland Club still exists, though it now allows entrance to Democrats, women, and cocktails.

Father and son are no doubt spinning in their (dry) graves.

## CHAPTER 13

# Charles W. Morse:
## *Serial Monopolist, Cheat,*
## *Liar, Swindler*

O h, where to begin? Could it be possible that from birth young Charles W. Morse was already a cool, calculating character with ice water in his veins? Given that he would one day be known as the Ice King, it's a safe bet that the wee Morse was a difficult tot prone to having his way. You have to give the man marks for staying the course: In all his seventy-seven years, he never deviated from that early chosen path.

As a young man, Charles worked for his father in the family's shipping business, which focused on pulling and pushing other people's loaded barges up and down the Kennebec River. His father, Capt. Benjamin Morse, started the Kennebec Towing Company and soon expanded it to include all manner of shipping, not just tugs and barges.

It was this company that young Morse eventually transformed into the moneymaking juggernaut Knickerbocker Towing Company after purchasing the Knickerbocker Ice Company. Soon he cornered the local ice trade by becoming the only outfit to tow ice locally, effectively monopolizing the market (and raising the price at the same time). The success of this simple but eminently effective method pleased Charles to no end. And it was a technique he would replicate to great effect a number of times in his long and storied career.

If Morse's father was a savvy businessman, his son hit that ball right out of the park. No one could accuse young Charles W. Morse of being a slouch where smart business practices were concerned. But couple those bold-stroke moves with unchecked greed

*Charles W. Morse, "The Ice King," monopolized shipping and banking, caused the Panic of 1907, lied his way out of prison, and amassed huge fortunes along the way.*

and insatiable hunger for power, and you have the makings of a man around whom others began to exercise caution.

Morse next ventured beyond the local business environs of the Kennebec River but received an annoying wake-up call. While on his home territory he was king of the waterways, making money hand over fist, but when his ships traveled to ports farther south, Morse was dismayed to find he had to pay a whole lot of money to other people to be towed into port. This didn't sit well with the calculating businessman, so he devised plans to tow his own loads the full distance. This necessitated a bigger fleet.

Undaunted, Morse looked around and saw opportunity where others saw dereliction and decay. He bought up numerous old tall ships, removed their masts and gutted them, effectively rendering those stately old schooners into barges with ample cargo capacity.

As business went, it was a smart move, for Morse was able to use one tugboat to pull three barges. Soon he commissioned custom-built, massive oceangoing barges built specifically for the task of hauling coastal loads. It proved to be the most profitable form of shipping to date, reducing transport costs by 50 percent. In the process, however, it rendered schooners nearly extinct. Since the barges didn't require big crews, Morse's tugs could drop them off for unloading then immediately head back up north for another load.

By the time Charles Morse reached the quarter-century mark, the young Mainer had wandered on down first to Boston, then on to the Big Apple to see what the big-city boys knew. And despite the fact that he was regarded as a bumpkin of the first order by none other than J. D. Rockefeller and J. P. Morgan, Morse did as he set out to do—earn more money in a year than he had up to that point in his young life, and then repeat the process ad infinitum. This he would do in short order—and for many years following, with no signs of slowing.

The upstart young businessman saw easy pickings in his path and continued on with his previous success in the ice business, replicating it in the major ports of the Northeastern coast. In 1897 he founded the Consolidated Ice Company and merged it two years later with a handful of other smaller ice-producing firms; from that emerged the American Ice Company. And since he hailed from Maine, a place where much of the ice of the day came from—having been cut from the state's many and plentiful rivers—he controlled not only the production of the ice but the shipment and sale of it as well.

Virtually overnight Morse doubled the price of ice to wholesalers and consumers and made himself and his backers many millions of dollars. At the same time he created a monopoly on ice in the greater New York region, earning himself the name the Ice King.

In 1900, a scandal arose due to his efforts to further increase the price of ice. But his intentions were exposed by the *New York Journal and Advertiser,* which revealed shady business relations, including favors and kickbacks, with New York City mayor Robert Van Wyck and notoriously crooked Tammany Hall boss Richard Croker, to whom Morse had given shares in his various ice holdings. This group of thieves was labeled as "the Ice Trust" in the press. After manipulating the stock, Morse managed to wriggle free of his ice-company holdings and emerged with a $12 million profit.

He married for a second time, his first wife having died in 1897 after bearing him three sons and a daughter. This time at the altar, he hitched up with Clemence Dodge, an Atlanta, Georgia, divorcée. They lived a lavish lifestyle, with a home on New York's Fifth Avenue and a summer home in Morse's hometown of Bath, Maine. But it was discovered that Dodge's first marriage had not been terminated legally, so her marriage to Charlie was annulled. Newspapers had a ball with the story, since Morse was already a very large public figure that the public loved to hate—he had, after all, affected nearly everyone in the greater New York City area by inflating ice prices. Eventually his marital status was resolved, and the Morses' marriage was restored.

He had at his fingertips assets in excess of $330 million and continued his monopolizing ways from back in the days of ice. But now it was not the river ice market the man was cornering but shipping.

Morse replicated his success in the ice biz by embarking on a calculated buying spree of a wide variety of shipping lines, consolidating them into larger companies. He bought up steamship lines from Maine down through the Gulf Coast. Long before leaving behind the moniker the Ice King, by 1907 Morse had earned the name Admiral of the Atlantic Coast, because he held virtually all coastal shipping from Maine to Texas in his chunky grip. And once again he held a monopoly, this time in coastal shipping, which affected goods and services vital to the daily operation of business and individuals all over the world.

The massive profits he realized from his shipping ventures allowed this so-called rube from Maine to gain a firm grip on the comings and goings of New York's throbbing economic heartbeat, namely banking. And nobody could take its pulse like Charles W. Morse. He soon held controlling shares in the National Bank of North America and the New Amsterdam National Bank and owned much of the Mercantile National Bank. His friendship with Montana copper king F. Augustus Heinze grew, and the pair of unscrupulous titans directed six national banks, nearly a dozen state banks, and numerous trust and insurance firms. The financial power they wielded was incredible. And what did they do with it? They worked to make more money and power for themselves, naturally. One of their schemes involved cornering the stock on copper. But their plan backfired, and depositors, sensing a crash, pulled their cash from Morse's banks, resulting in the Panic of 1907.

Within five days, by October 20, 1907, the New York Clearing House put a stop to Morse's greedy ploy—for the time being—by forcing him to resign his banking positions. He was strongly persuaded by a committee of fifteen Wall Streeters, who enacted a big-banking form of vigilante justice: sell up, get out of town, and keep the hell out of their business, namely banking.

But the damage had already been done, and nationwide fiscal panic ensued. Morse's holdings, including shipping, went into receivership, and many of his assets were sold off to help pay for his misdeeds.

In November 1908, Morse was indicted, convicted, and sentenced to fifteen years in an Atlanta, Georgia, federal prison. His crimes: falsifying books of his bank and misuse of bank funds. He stayed out on appeal, but despite the incessant and heavily funded efforts of his team of attorneys, he ran out of appeal time. On January 2, 1910, off went Morse to prison. He wailed, he gnashed his teeth, he growled and shouted to the press as he was led from the courthouse: "There is no one on Wall Street who is not doing what I have done! . . . The administration wanted a scapegoat."

So how then, if he was guilty of so much fraud and convicted and sentenced to fifteen years, did C. W. Morse manage to spend only two years in the clink? Well, once a lord of fraud . . . Morse hired big-gun attorney Harry M. Daugherty and, along with a $5,000 retainer, gave him strict orders to do whatever he had to do to get him out of prison. The driven lawyer tried every trick in the book, but President William Howard Taft said no-go.

Undaunted, Daugherty brought in a raft of medical experts to examine Morse, but they declared the man sound as a bell. The persistent Daugherty called in a different batch of doctors. And this time he struck gold. Why, said the docs, that poor Morse is in wretched condition. Among other illnesses and complaints, they found he was suffering from Bright's disease, an ailment in which the kidneys are inflamed. In Morse's condition, the doctors determined, he would not see another year.

How could this be? Simple. Before the medical examination, Morse imbibed a tonic of chemical-laced soap, the effects of which mimicked Bright's disease. Bowing to pressure for leniency in light of Morse's imminent demise, President Taft put pen to paper, and Morse was soon pardoned and on his way to Wiesbaden, Germany, for treatment.

An interesting side-note: One of Morse's fellow prisoners in Georgia was, appropriately enough, none other than the ultimate fraudster Charles Ponzi, inventor of the Ponzi scheme, which has been used in various guises over the years by the unscrupulous to bilk massive amounts of money from massive numbers of people.

One wonders what pointers Morse picked up while in the big house with such a like-minded fellow.

Before Morse had been sprung, when he had first hired Daugherty to find a means of getting him out of jail, Morse had promised the lawyer an additional $25,000 once he was out. Now that Morse was safely ensconced in Germany, he reneged on his deal with the attorney. Not a wise move considering Daugherty was well connected in Washington, DC.

President Taft found himself in the news, explaining to reporters how he'd been hoodwinked. But a presidential pardon doesn't come easy, and it doesn't easily come undone. And so Morse made his way back to the States, free as a bird, healthy as a horse, and rubbing his hands together in anticipation of making more money with other people's money. It is also presumed he reluctantly paid Daugherty the money owed him.

However, the duper soon got a taste of his own medicine, a tincture he decided he did not at all like. Before his trial, Morse allegedly signed the titles of a number of his assets, including ships, to a fellow Mainer, banker and presumed friend Walter Reid, who had assured his friend that he would protect C. W.'s investments and, when Morse got out of prison, Morse would regain control of them. But when Morse came around with his hand out, looking for his vessels, Reid drew a blank look and asked what ships ol' Charlie boy might be talking about.

It didn't take Morse long to be back in the glare of an unwanted spotlight. In the summer of 1915, his shipping company, Hudson Navigation, was sued for unfair competitive practices. It didn't seem to faze him, because within months he unveiled his latest empiric idea: the United States Shipbuilding Company. In reality it was a multilayered cake of sixteen small companies, each in possession of just one steamship. He sold stock in the company via a scheme involving the US mail—a scheme that would later earn him an indictment by the government.

But any such worries were light-years away for Morse, who saw rosy business opportunities with the US involvement in World

War I. He managed to grease enough Capitol Hill palms to land thirty-six shipbuilding contracts. Based on the strength of these government contracts alone, he borrowed money from yet another government arm and purchased the necessary facilities and materials. Morse was nothing if not brazen.

His firms ended up building twenty-two of the thirty-six contracted ships before the war reached its end, and orders for the remaining contracted ships were canceled. When the war dust settled and the Justice Department delved into possible war frauds, you'll never guess whose name popped up time and time again.

Ol' Charlie managed to be sitting squarely in the hot seat once again. He was charged with overselling his facilities' abilities and was also found to have helped himself to money for personal gain that had been intended, per the contracts, for shipbuilding. He also hadn't been up front about his wartime profiteering, of which he was decidedly guilty. In 1921, his Hudson Navigation Company went bankrupt, and Charlie was indicted for war profiteering and fraud, if not for being a jerk.

Once again, Morse proved fleet of foot. He headed to France, but he wasn't there long before he received a cable from the attorney general of the US Department of Justice demanding that he return. And who was that annoying attorney general? None other than Morse's old lawyer, Harry Daugherty.

Court case piled upon court case, and Morse spent much of the early 1920s dodging, parrying, and thrusting, doing his best to keep one shiny boot ahead of the law. Though he was ultimately acquitted of the profiteering charges, he had to face the music on a 1925 civil suit brought against his Virginia Shipbuilding Company by the US government. He lost the suit and was forced to pay $11.5 million.

By 1926, Charles W. Morse had grown financially weak and physically and mentally weary. His wife, Clemence, died in July of that year. What charges remained pending against him, including those stemming from the mail fraud case against his United States Shipbuilding Company, were dropped. By early September,

Morse was unable to handle his own affairs, and his sons had him declared mentally incompetent. A guardian was appointed to see to his needs.

He was remembered in his last days as a sickly old man wheeled about his Maine hometown of Bath by a male nurse. But sick as he was, Morse still managed to conjure up bawdy whistles whenever he was wheeled past a lady on the streets of Bath. By January 12, 1933, he'd reached the end of his tether. After a series of strokes and episodes of pneumonia, the Ice King died, a man broken in mind and body who left a long smoking trail of financial wreckage behind.

His propensity for never having enough of the challenge of the chase is what often marks a truly successful person. Unfortunately, in Charles W. Morse, it was a trait twinned with greed and disregard for others.

One wonders how much young folks today roaming the halls of Charles W. Morse High School in Bath, Maine, know of the man for whom their school is named—and who donated the money to have it built.

It could be easily believed that the popular 1903 board game, Monopoly, was secretly based on the exploits of Charles W. Morse, who was operating at the peak of his monopolization in 1903 when the game was introduced. And that portly rascal, Rich Uncle Pennybags, the mascot of the game, could well be modeled on that top-hatted tyrant, Charles W. Morse. The resemblance is easy to see—especially when he's grinning greedily and clutching sacks of other people's money—and most especially when he must venture to jail with all haste, something his creditors took great relish in pointing out. Good thing for Morse and Morse wannabes that there's that "get out of jail free" card. After all, it worked for Morse back in 1912.

## CHAPTER 14

# Judge John Pickering:
## *Drunk, Insane, Impeached!*

Poor John Pickering. . . . Where to begin? Chief among his numerous offenses is that he was never around when needed. Just what was Judge Pickering doing that was more important than tending to the federal business to which no less a personage than George Washington appointed him?

He was drinking—liquor, booze, the demon alcohol. And due to his drinking, he slowly unraveled mentally. Or it might be that he was already well on his way to mental instability when he took to the bottle. No matter which came first, boozy bottle or mental mottle, Pickering will forever be remembered as the first of thirteen federal judges to be impeached (to date—there's still time for more!).

Born in Newington, New Hampshire, on September 22, 1737, Pickering began his professional life as an idealistic young man filled with promise (it is said that he spoke twenty languages). A Harvard graduate of the class of 1761, Pickering decided against a career as a clergyman, opting instead on pursuing a life in law. He felt that he could effect more and better change for his fellow man if he were able to offer legal recourse to those most in need.

His early years of private practice first began in Greenland, New Hampshire, then Portsmouth. During this difficult time, he barely scraped together enough recompense from his low-budget clients to keep his growing family clothed and fed.

In 1783 he was elected to the New Hampshire state legislature for four years before devoting himself to his private practice once again until 1790. In 1787 he was chosen to represent New Hampshire as a member of that state's delegation to the Continental Congress in Philadelphia. But because he had a lifelong

*If he could be bothered to show up for work at all, Judge John Pickering, the first federal official to be impeached, frequently screamed drunken obscenities from the bench before passing out.*

and increasingly disabling hypochondria with a special aversion to crossing water, Pickering declined to attend, as the journey would require him to cross a number of rivers. Despite this, he was one of the signers of his state's own constitution, and his was the first state to craft and adopt one.

From 1790 to 1795, he served as chief justice for what was then called "the New Hampshire Superior Court of Judicature," but he began to succumb to bouts of a strange illness—drinking binges and hangovers—that became more frequent, enough so that a number of people pushed to have him removed from the position. But once again, as it is wont to do, politics intervened and sullied the process of logic.

As an alternate solution, New Hampshire officials contacted George Washington and asked him to reappoint Pickering to the position of judge of the US District Court for the District of New Hampshire, a court that saw very few cases at the time. It was hoped that with such a decrease in his workload, perhaps poor Pickering might find the time to once again regain his wits and wring out his liver.

Oddly enough, the job switch seemed to do the trick—for a time, at least. No cerebral slouch, Pickering must surely have known he was on a downhill slide should he continue his negligent ways. He appeared to buck up, kept his drinking to a manageable level, and served tolerably well for a few years. By 1800, however, poor Pickering had once again begun to slip in his duties, this time worse than ever before.

He'd resumed his previously spotty practice of failing to attend court, the very court he was charged with overseeing. The lawyers, defendants, plaintiffs, and juries would all assemble—only to be stymied in their pursuit of justice by the distinct lack of a judge.

The clerk of courts was forced to repeatedly enter one comment into his records: "This court was adjourned, due to absence of judge."

That little foible would be bad enough, but when Pickering did finally deign to appear in court, he behaved in a most bizarre manner that his beleaguered underlings attributed to his creeping alcoholism. At increasingly frequent times, poor pickled Pickering weaved and wobbled at the bench, not even bothering to keep an eye on his court. He sometimes fell asleep during the judicial process.

More often than not, however, Pickering raved drunkenly and loudly through the proceedings. He swore, blasphemed, and shrieked at anyone he could fix with his rheumy gaze. This, as one might guess, did not make for a courtroom atmosphere conducive to getting done the work of upholding the law.

As such episodes increased in frequency, public rumblings grew louder, enough so that on April 25, 1801, the clerk of the New Hampshire district court staff wrote to the court's overseeing body, the US Court of Appeals for the First Circuit. He requested a replacement judge, if only temporarily, stating that Judge Pickering had gone insane:

> *To the Honorable the Judges of the Circuit Court of the United States for the First Circuit now sitting at Portsmouth within and for the District of New Hampshire this 25th day of April Anno Domini 1801 — Humbly sheweth the Subscriber — that the District Judge of the District Court for said derangement — is at this time incapable of performing the duties of his office. Wherefor he suggests to this Honorable Court the necessity of directing one of the Circuit Judges of said Court to perform the duties of said District Judge within and for said District Judge within and for said District during the period the inability of said District Judge shall continue.*

The First Circuit Court of Appeals sent circuit judge Jeremiah Smith as a temporary replacement. Smith sat the bench on Pickering's behalf for the duration of the 1801 session. The following March 1802, Judge Pickering showed up as promised—then immediately adjourned the court until the following day. Once again lawyers, staff, and the public wrinkled their noses at the man's boozy reek, rolled their eyes, and hoped for the best.

The next day came and—to no one's great surprise—there was no sign of Pickering. He had once again pulled his now-famous vanishing trick. From there his attendance record grew worse by the minute, as did any defense, however diminishing, he might have had remaining about his sanity. Miraculously Pickering managed—or rather his staff enabled him—to stumble, snooze, rant, and booze his way through the spring, summer, and into the fall.

By November 1802 the inevitable finally came to pass as the case that finished Pickering's career once and for all turned up on the docket: *United States v. The Eliza*. Captain Ladd of the impounded ship *Eliza* was summoned to court to pay tax on a boatload of what he swore was used cable, not new, as tax collector Whipple claimed. Whipple had seized the ship, stating Ladd had violated revenue laws.

The district attorney and the arresting officer were both Republicans, whereas the defendant, Ladd, and his attorney were Federalists. In fact, Ladd was the son of an influential and wealthy Federalist family. Judge John Pickering also happened to be a dyed-in-the-wool Federalist.

The trial's opening arguments kicked off bright and early on the morning of November 11, 1802. Pickering promptly approved a motion to adjourn for the day, stating, "I shall be sober tomorrow. I am now damned drunk."

Wonder of wonders, he did show up for work the next day, and without hearing any witnesses for the prosecution—the government—Pickering found in favor of Ladd. The district attorney immediately called him on this breach of courtroom etiquette, pointing out that Pickering had yet to hear any of the DA's witnesses.

Pickering leaned out over the bench and said, "You may bring forty thousand [witnesses] and they will not alter the decree." After this, he ordered the ship and its questionable cargo returned to its captain.

The district attorney and tax collector Whipple, seething with rage, formally requested assistance from government officials to have Pickering removed from his position. Whipple was convinced that Pickering had ruled as he did solely because Ladd's family and Pickering shared such strong Federalist tendencies.

That was all President Thomas Jefferson, an avowed Federalist hater, needed to hear. For too long he had been inundated with complaints about New Hampshire's drunken, deranged judge, and he had been looking for any excuse to oust the man. After all, in Jefferson's purview, there was nothing worse than a drunken, insane federal judge—unless he happened to be a drunken, insane *Federalist* federal judge. Now he finally had the ideal excuse to rid himself of two burrs under his saddle, which is just what President Jefferson went about doing.

According to the US Constitution, provision for removal of a judge is based on "impeachment for, and Conviction of, Treason, Bribery or other high Crimes and Misdemeanors." A potential sticking point was that the Constitution made no provision for removal of a mentally addled federal judge. Pickering had enough wit left to know this, and he refused to resign his position.

A Washington war began to rage in which Federalists accused Jefferson's administration of attempting to undermine the Constitution—the Republicans had already repealed the Judiciary Act of 1801. Federalists felt sure that should Republicans succeed in removing Pickering from office they would harm the precarious balance of power between the judicial branch and Congress. And if Pickering lost his position, a Republican would most likely assume his seat on the bench, and the Federalists would be on even shakier governmental ground.

By February 1803, Jefferson (of the Jeffersonian Democrat-Republicans) urged the Jeffersonian-controlled US House of Representatives to impeach Pickering. This they formally did March 2, 1803, on the charges of unlawful rulings and drunkenness.

Later that year, the December 30, 1803, edition of the *Journal of the House of Representatives of the United States* stated:

*That whereas for the due, faithful, and impartial admin-*
*istration of justice, temperance and sobriety are essential*
*qualities in the character of a judge, yet the said John*
*Pickering, being a man of loose morals and intemperate*
*habits, on the 11th and 12th days of November, in the year*
*1802, being then judge of the district court in and for the*
*district of New Hampshire, did appear on the bench of the*
*said court for the administration of justice in a state of*
*total intoxication, produced by the free and intemperate*
*use of intoxicating liquors; and did then and there fre-*
*quently, in a most profane and indecent manner, invoke*
*the name of the Supreme Being, to the evil example of all*
*the good citizens of the United States; and was then and*
*there guilty of other high misdemeanors, disgraceful to*
*his own character as a judge and degrading to the honor*
*of the United States.*

It would take the Senate a year before it instigated its own hearings and subsequent trial.

As with so many episodes in Pickering's life, his impeachment trial promised to be anything but a neat and tidy affair, primarily because the potential for much political game-playing lay behind it. After all, the Jeffersonians and the Federalists were too eager to lock horns, one wanting to maintain a firm hold on ground gained and secure even more, and one not wanting to cede that ground.

It was a long, rough year for poor pickled Pickering, and not surprisingly, he slipped deeper into drunkenness and lunacy. Incredibly, despite his obvious failings, he was allowed to hold his judicial position during that year, though by title only, as his court did not convene. By the time his Senate impeachment trial began, on March 12, 1804, Pickering was in no condition to travel—not that he would have anyway, since the journey would necessitate crossing rivers, and that phobia had only increased over the years. So he sent his son, Jacob Pickering, to speak on his behalf before the United States Senate.

The younger Pickering's argument, it turns out, was not much of an argument at all. Instead he concurred that, yes, his father was indeed insane. But, argued Jacob, that didn't mean the old man should be impeached, for heaven's sake.

As the hearings progressed, Jeffersonians, who outnumbered the Federalists and enjoyed a healthy majority, provided much of the evidence to support an impeachment. It turns out that the case was built largely on the man's behavior during the Ladd trial.

The Jeffersonians alleged that during those proceedings Pickering had been repeatedly and debilitatingly inebriated and deranged. His son and the few others who spoke on Judge Pickering's behalf had little useful defense, as these allegations were impossible to refute. The Ladd trial had been attended by sober professionals and numerous others, who had all witnessed the timeworn Pickering debacle.

John Quincy Adams weighed in with the question of the day: "The dilemma is between the determination to remove the man on impeachment for high crimes and misdemeanors, though he be insane."

On March 12, 1804, of thirty-four senators, twenty-six were in attendance. Nineteen Republicans found Judge John Pickering guilty of all charges, whereas seven Federalists voted to acquit. The result, though it represented a bare minimum of a two-thirds vote, found Judge Pickering convicted of all charges leveled against him. He was thus formally impeached, becoming the first federally appointed officer to be impeached by a guilty verdict.

Meanwhile, the court over which he had presided had not met for two years, nearly to the day. On June 19, 1804, Pickering's replacement, Republican district attorney John Samuel Sherburne, heard his first case.

John Pickering, now disgraced as well as drunk and more insane than ever, lasted little more than a year following his trial. He expired on April 11, 1805, in Portsmouth, New Hampshire.

Being this country's first federal official to be impeached is a dismal distinction, especially considering Pickering's early promise and long years of dedication to providing low-cost legal assistance for the poor. It should also be remembered that he worked hard to ensure that his beloved New Hampshire became a state in 1788 with proper legal safeguards for its citizens in place in its constitution, of which Pickering was a signer. Sadly, these strong points of his character will nonetheless forever be overshadowed by his propensity for strong drink, and his ravings from the bench.

## CHAPTER 15

# Isaac Hill & William Loeb III:
## *Crotchety Newsmen*

Though separated by a century and, in party name at least, opposing sides of the political spectrum, Isaac Hill and William Loeb III were both powerful and influential New Hampshire newspapermen. They also shared the dubious distinction of being widely disliked. It seems each was perpetually annoyed with life and chose to vent his wrath on others.

The first of the two men regarded herein to sit on the throne of cantankerous editor in New Hampshire was Isaac Hill. And boy was he a curmudgeon. He might well have qualified as the king of all curmudgeons. The man was an odious, unpleasant bully who used the powerful presence of his newspaper—and a formidable skill with words—to bludgeon his perceived enemies into submission or silence. One wonders if he started out life that way.

Isaac Hill began his days on April 6, 1788, in West Cambridge, Massachusetts, the firstborn of an impoverished farming family. As the oldest of nine, providing for the family fell to Isaac, who was but fourteen when his father lost his sanity. The old man's descent into madness thrust his large brood into even worse straits. An accident on the farm left young Isaac with a limp and a lifelong predisposition to frailty. If his body was impaired, his mind made up for it.

In 1802, at age fourteen, he apprenticed to a newspaper publisher and printing office, home of the *Cabinet* newspaper in Amherst, New Hampshire, in hopes that he might learn the ropes. Never was a more appropriate match made. Spare moments were filled with reading any book he could lay a hand on, and in this manner he educated himself. Within a few years he had developed a mastery of the printing and publishing game.

*Before Isaac Hill became a crotchety politician, he was a crotchety newspaperman with a fierce reputation for skewering friend and foe alike in print.*

COURTESY US SENATE HISTORICAL OFFICE

Along the way he had also formed definite opinions about politics, about commerce, and about how the common man should and should not be treated. By the time Hill was twenty-one in 1809, the *American Patriot* newspaper, a weekly based in Concord, the new state capital town of New Hampshire, had fallen on hard times and was up for sale at a reduced rate.

With the encouragement of friends and a $300 loan, Hill purchased the sinking newspaper, moved himself to Concord, and promptly renamed the rag the *New Hampshire Patriot.* His first issue was a four-pager that from day one laid out the young upstart's political intent. Hill swung for the bleachers, not caring a whit whom he might injure in the process. He addressed that first diatribe "To the Public," and for the next one thousand words Hill made himself into the defender of the common man, a voice for the laborer, which immediately set him at odds with the local wealthy elite.

All of this sounds admirable, not the actions nor the coming up through the ranks of a man looking to curry favor. What it was not, however, was kind in the least. From the start Hill was combative, antagonistic, and petty. This approach was intentional and did not differ much from that of other newspapers of the day, which frequently were little more than party-run instruments for spreading propaganda. Hill was after a visceral response from readers. He wanted to touch them hard and leave an imprint. He did that—and more.

Hill was a hardcore Democrat in the Jacksonian mold, and as editor of the *Patriot,* this surly, pucker-faced man with the perpetual visage of annoyance and perturbation had a strange habit of stalking about town clad in his ink-stained printer's clothes long after he outgrew the need to do so. He considered the ink stains a hard-earned badge of honor. Pride in one's chosen pursuit is no crime, but using the venerable role of a newspaperman to savage people in print . . . not so noble.

Hill did not limit his innate distrust to politicians but spread the enmity democratically and frequently across the pages of his newspaper. Despite his own political agenda, which he wore as proudly as the ink stains on his sleeve—pro common man, pro low taxes, and pro small government, views shared by many at the time—Hill nonetheless managed to lash out at common folk and high rollers alike, and for all manner of reasons. Among his pet topics was the biggest one of the day—the emergence of railroads and their growth across the New England region.

A number of times his upstart editorializing instigated extreme anger, resulting in physical confrontations on the street. Though his beloved common man seemed to be squarely in his corner, Hill was so persuasive and yet vitriolic at the same time that he was often accused of having powers of witchcraft and was thought to have descended from Salem's more notorious residents.

Those who knew of his father's madness wondered if perhaps young Isaac wasn't so much idealistic as insane. No doubt such comments stung Hill, but he had a habit of feigning surprise at the vehement reactions he incited, explaining his editorial diatribes as attempts at self-defense.

For the next two decades, Hill, decidedly anti-Federalist, vigorously supported the Jeffersonians. The *Patriot* served as an unabashed mouthpiece for the leading lights of the party, and many of its higher-ups contributed regularly to its pages. With each successive year Hill's power, influence, and status in state, regional, and national politics strengthened and flourished.

He was petty in his attacks, and as time rolled on and his paper's popularity grew—largely because of his sensationalistic and sniping style—so did his sphere of influence. Politicians who one week might be skewered in his pages either shunned him and suffered his broadly read barbs or simpered for forgiveness and positive coverage the next.

Despite his workaholic tendencies, Hill found time to marry Susanna Ayer, a member of one of the state's most respected families, with whom he had four children, two of whom, sons, followed him in the newspaper trade. He was also a savvy businessman, purchasing real estate throughout the greater Concord region. His land holdings allowed him to assume control of all New Hampshire mail routes, ensuring he distributed his newspaper for free. He also became a scion of a number of institutions—he helped found Concord's first Episcopal church, became director of the local agricultural society, helped found Merrimack County, and made Concord its seat.

All of these were mere dalliances compared with his burgeoning interest in politics. It was affairs of state that kept his juices flowing. But if friends and foes alike thought they would be spared his sharp tongue, they had another thing coming.

At the state level he was elected to the position of clerk of the House of Representatives in 1819 and again in 1825. He also served as a New Hampshire state senator for two different terms, first from 1820 to 1823, and again from 1827 to 1828.

As secretary of New Hampshire's Republican committee, he wielded increasingly intense political power and doled out jobs to those individuals he favored. Likewise, he continued to use his newspaper for venting his spleen on anyone who dared cross him.

Those early political positions, it seems, were ideal training for his zealous support of Andrew Jackson's bid for the White House against incumbent John Quincy Adams in 1828–29. As a hero from the War of 1812, Jackson exemplified the common-man approach to politics that Hill so revered.

In January 1828, the thirteenth anniversary of Jackson's victory at the Battle of New Orleans, Hill made sure New Hampshire resounded with pro-Jackson chest-thumping, speechifying, balls, parades, and statewide celebrations. It didn't matter that Jackson was not in attendance, as Hill had spun the day to be so much bigger than any one person. By the time Hill delivered a fiery speech that evening in Concord, describing Jackson as "the second savior of our country," everyone felt sure that Old Hickory himself had already won the election.

Hill cranked up the rhetoric machine and made darn sure that his readers perceived then-current President Adams as a low and loathsome creature. He bizarrely referred to Adams as pimp to

Alexander I, when Adams had held the position of ambassador to Russia. Hill's fanatical rhetoric traveled nationwide and contributed mightily to Jackson's success.

In 1828 this strong unwavering support for Andrew Jackson's successful bid for the White House earned Hill a spot on the new president's fabled Kitchen Cabinet, a collection of close friends and associates who had as much or more influence on the president than did his own official advisors.

Hill sold his newspaper in 1829 and was appointed as second comptroller of the National Treasury by Jackson, though without Senate confirmation. He served in the position from 1829 to 1830, when the Senate refused to give him the official nod. So he ran for the US Senate seat from his home state of New Hampshire and won the election, serving from 1831 until 1836, when he shifted his attention to his state's governor's race. He won that battle and served as New Hampshire's twenty-third governor from 1836 to 1839.

Following his stint as governor, Hill served a year working in Boston as the US subtreasurer before turning his attention in 1841 back to publishing with the *Farmer's Monthly Visitor,* a newspaper he had owned since 1835. At this time he also began dipping his inky digits into real estate speculation and banking. Also during these years, he gained control of the Concord Railroad Corporation and suddenly found himself selling out his ideals, his common-man attitudes, for the sake of financial gain.

When he returned from Washington, DC, he tried to purchase his old newspaper, the *Patriot.* But he'd sold his stake in it back when he entered the US Senate in 1831, and the new owners had continued to make a go of it. They weren't interested in having him back in control—it's not difficult to wonder why.

So he did what any bitter curmudgeon would do: He sued them. But the judge said no dice and left Hill to snarl and prattle on in the pages of his new newspaper, the predictably named *Hill's New Hampshire Patriot.* In those pages, he continued to howl and rage about his pet peeves and his political proclivities. But whereas before he had had some level of support from his public, albeit a begrudging, bullied one, this time around the entire political climate of the nation, and certainly that of New Hampshire (and the Concord region in particular), had changed enough that his anger no longer seemed relevant. The public had grown tired of being bullied and yelled at by Isaac Hill, and Hill, too, began to weary of his own voice echoing back at him from a public who no longer was willing to swallow the bitter pills he peddled.

His dour mood aside, Isaac Hill's accomplishments are long and impressive. Though he was respected, if not liked, by a good many people in New Hampshire and in Washington, there were many more who downright despised him. And apparently the feeling was mutual.

He spent much of his life and energy devoted to politics and political causes and fights, but Isaac Hill first and foremost considered himself a newspaperman. His form of journalism was a far cry from objective, but then again much journalism at the time was such. And as editor in chief, he wasn't afraid of editorializing all over the place. He would no doubt be pleased to note that today New Hampshire's popular independent daily, the *Concord Monitor,* can trace its roots back to Hill's *New Hampshire Patriot.*

He died on March 22, 1851, while in Washington, DC, and is buried at the Blossom Hill Cemetery in Concord, New Hampshire.

Long before he became a conservative New England newspaper tycoon, William Loeb III's private life was a series of trainwreck relationships and double crosses. He alienated his father (who had been an executive secretary to Theodore Roosevelt)— and got himself removed from the old man's will—early on by marrying a woman his folks disapproved of. Later he took great pains to hide the six-year marriage.By the mid-1940s he had purchased a number of newspapers in Vermont and New Hampshire, and his public life was well on its way to rivaling that of his private. His papers were filled with angry rants and deceits that often stemmed from his attempts at obfuscating the facts.

Not surprisingly, Loeb claimed he suffered from ulcers, which kept him out of active duty during World War II. Through a variety of roller-coaster episodes—an extramarital affair; newspaper purchases; loans from mommy; another divorce; a monopolization of media in New Hampshire that included newspapers and controlling interest in a television station; and marriage to his third wife, Elizabeth "Nackey" Scripps-Gallowhur, herself granddaughter of famous newspaper publisher E. W. Scripps—Loeb remained a staunch ultraconservative voice in American media.

He was also staunchly conservative in his business practices as well. In 1949, he famously canned the crew at his Vermont-based newspapers when they attempted to unionize. That same year, Loeb was sued by his own mother in 1949 for $1 million. She was angry that he would have dared to dally with Nackey (herself still married) while he still had a wife (and child). Years later, when his wealthy mother died, Loeb had been cut out of her will.

Not surprisingly, he sued, demanding 75 percent of the estate, even though his numerous siblings and other named recipients were also in line to receive estate funds. The suit dragged on for five years, reached Vermont's Supreme Court, and nearly emptied the old woman's coffers. Loeb ended up with 10 percent of the all-but-depleted funds. He was caught in a number of outright fabrications throughout his career, often wedged into his front-page editorials. Among them, his claim that he had worked as a reporter on the *New York World,* though no record of his employment existed. He even listed his dates of employ as being nearly a decade after the paper folded.

Professionally the man was an acrimonious, conservative powerhouse, responsible over the years for shaking up nationally known public and private figures. In his numerous front-page editorials and red-faced diatribes, he often resorted to cheap-shot name-calling to get his point across. Unfortunately his tactics were effective.

In print, Loeb referred to President Dwight D. Eisenhower as "that stinking hypocrite," and in an editorial in June 1955, he also famously wrote, "This newspaper now solemnly charges that President Eisenhower has done more to destroy the respect, honor and power of the United States than any President in its history."

He referred to President John F. Kennedy as "the No. 1 liar in the USA" and to Henry Kissinger as "Kissinger the Kike." In another famous episode, Loeb was allegedly responsible for halting the 1972 presidential bid of Maine senator Edmund S. Muskie (to whom Loeb referred in 1968 as "Moscow Muskie") by helping to fabricate the famous "Canuck letter." This forged document addressed to the press appeared in Loeb's *Union Leader* newspaper, claiming that Muskie was bigoted against French Canadians and that Muskie's wife was overly fond of booze—both outright lies. And in the 1970s Loeb also savaged the teenage daughter of New Hampshire governor Walter Peterson Jr. in print for her support of marijuana reform.

Loeb was a heavy-handed bully whose personal and professional actions are the stuff of nightmares and headaches. Did the world really need his viciousness and vitriol? Surely a man with Loeb's obvious talent for journalistic persuasion could have figured out a way to express himself without sniping and screaming in print. William Loeb III left behind a memorable legacy, to be sure, but one to be proud of? Hardly.

## CHAPTER 16

# Seth Wyman:
## *Self-Professed Pathological Pilferer*

In the opening lines of his 1843 autobiography, *The Life and Adventures of Seth Wyman: Embodying the Principal Events of a Life Spent in Robbery, Theft, Gambling, Passing Counterfeit Money, etc., etc. (Written by Himself.)*, self-proclaimed sleazy swindler and thief extraordinaire Seth Wyman explains why he so magnanimously decided to pen his life story, from prison, for all the world to read:

> *In presenting the following record of crime and folly to the reader, I am aware that I disobey the promptings of selfishness, which would forever confine the succeeding details within my own breast, and thus cause them to die with their author; but a sense of justice due the world, with a desire that a life which has been worse than useless, may yet prove a benefit to the coming generation in deterring them from travelling the same thorny path which I have trod, urges me to lay them before the world.*

Oh, spare us, Mr. Wyman! And yet, as difficult as it is to stomach the weasel's selfless, martyr-like tone, especially considering his book's subtitle, the deeper one reads into the book, the more one finds it increasingly difficult to wholly despise the man. Sure, he was a jerk. By his own admission, he was an unrepentant jerk. But in print he's also an endearing and fascinating jerk.

Published in Manchester, New Hampshire, in 1845 by J. H. Cate, Printer, the book delivers exactly what the title says it will. And reading it is similar to watching a car wreck—over and over and over. Wyman is a freak show and a soap opera all in one.

THE

# LIFE AND ADVENTURES

OF

# SETH WYMAN,

# EMBODYING

THE

PRINCIPAL EVENTS OF A LIFE SPENT IN
ROBBERY, THEFT, GAMBLING, PASS-
ING COUNTERFEIT MONEY, &c., &c.

## WRITTEN BY HIMSELF.

MANCHESTER, N. H.
J. H. CATE, PRINTER.
1843.

*Seth Wyman's incredible life of larceny began as a tot
and didn't let up for the rest of his days.*

He can't seem to help himself from indulging in his obsessions. Whereas most of us tend to do this with beer or cupcakes, Wyman did so with thievery.

Wyman also might provide the answer to the age-old question: Are jerks born, or are they made? In Seth Wyman's case, it seems as if he were born for the task, on what we must assume was a blustery, bleak March 4, 1784, in Goffstown, New Hampshire, to Sarah and Seth Wyman. He says of himself, "Almost from the cradle [I] was addicted to mischief and roguery."

And speaking of tasks, what a lifelong chore he must have been to his mother and father. To his credit, it seems he knew this, for he frequently refers to them in endearing terms, and perhaps with a hint of regret. But as the book progresses, the reader realizes regret isn't something Wyman conveys convincingly in the least. Glee, perhaps, at being a thief, but regret? Scarcely.

Early in the book he lavishes praise on both his parents and their kindly demeanors: "I leave the contradictions between the character of both my parents and my own, to be accounted for by those philosophers who assert that the moral condition of the offspring depends upon that of their progenitors."

Wyman's illustrious career as a lifelong jerk all began, as such stories do, way back when he was a lad. His earliest recollected episode of thievery sets the course for much of Wyman's life: While accompanying his mother to a neighbor's house, he spied a shiny coin on a dresser; ensuring that no one was around, the wily youth determined the coin would be his. He was nothing if not premeditating in his pilfering.

Young Wyman found a stool, shoved it over to the tall piece of furniture, scrambled up, pocketed his prize, and set everything to rights again. He tells how he had already concocted a plan to drop the coin on the road as they walked home, whereupon little Seth would "find" the cold, hard cash. This he did, and the money was his. He palmed it with a grin and never looked back.

Soon he evolved a straightforward set of guiding pilfering principles: "Nothing was valued by me unless I had succeeded in pilfering it from some other person, and the more trouble I was obliged to take in stealing an article, the higher I valued it. And I always carefully preserved such things as memorials of my skill and success."

He frequently pinched chains, axes, and other items from neighbors' sheds, then told the victims he'd found the items. The relieved neighbors would out of courtesy offer the boy a reward. He would boldly request six coppers—and in this way he began to "earn" money for himself. Wyman justified thievery because, he says, he "disliked exertion." Who doesn't?

On being told by his parents that girdling a tree—stripping it around its trunk—would kill it, and furthermore that it was an offense punishable by law, Wyman says, "This was sufficient inducement for me to undertake it immediately." And he did, first performing it on a neighbor's six apple trees; he was elated to find that the trees subsequently died. He was further thrilled to find that though a large reward was placed for the capture of the offender, no one found him out.

He continued on in this manner, killing trees and deriving great satisfaction from the wanton act. "I was never discovered, however, and was considerably elated by my success. I continued the amusement of killing trees for some time undiscovered." He was eventually caught savaging a large white oak with an axe. Growing mighty proud of his developing proficiency at lying, he talked his way out of a flogging.

Wyman also stole two of his father's game traps, set them, then proceeded to rise early each morning and steal from his father's traps as well as his neighbors. No one caught on, leaving him with much fur to sell. ("I procured fur enough to buy me a suit of clothes, and I felt proud of my skill and success in roguery.") He also stole money and trinkets at local militia gatherings and fruit from neighbors—he took nearly anything that wasn't nailed down. And if it was and he took a shine to it, he found a way to pry it loose and pocket it.

As a teenager, he abhorred work and any pursuits other than his two most abiding passions: "There were only two kinds of business, which I could follow with any kind of pleasure, or even patience, namely: keeping company with the girls, and thieving."

By the time he reached young adulthood, he began to become suspected in local and then far-ranging, larger-scale thievings, all of which he was guilty, naturally. Court appearances became more frequent, and his innocence harder won with each.

In reference to this period in his life, Wyman waxes long and eloquent about his various amorous pursuits and encounters: "I believe, however, that I broke no hearts, for both parties the latter seemed an unnecessary appendage." Certainly that sentiment should give readers a clue as to the sort of young ladies with whom he associated.

One of these dalliances resulted in a breach of promise for marriage and an ensuing pregnancy. Wyman denied paternity, though admitted in his book that "she was right." She swore before a judge, and he was found guilty and had to pay $120. He gave the matter no thought from then on and seemed only pleased and proud that he was able to once more squirm his way out of the constrictions of responsibility.

Wyman also did not lack in self-confidence—his ego runs unchecked throughout the lengthy book. His opinion of himself, his looks, and his various skills are almost comical in their forthright cockiness. Taken in context, remarks of his matter-of-fact confidence about his own abilities draw the reader into Wyman's ken of personal opinion: "I had naturally considerable mechanical skill." He refers to himself a number of times as "a young man rather good-looking."

But none of that holds a candle to Wyman's apparent mastery of the fine art of pugilism. If anyone doubted Wyman's ability to embroider a yarn, he need only read the numerous purple-prose accounts of the violent episodes that happened repeatedly throughout his life.

In these narratives, Wyman frequently finds himself hard pressed by bullies when he is looking for little more than an innocent bit of refreshment. And yet each time he takes careful pains to tell us that he gave better than he got, as with the thrashing he delivered to a blacksmith: "I sprang upon him and pummeled his head and face, until the men, fearing I should kill him, pulled me off. His face was pounded out of all natural form, into a mere jelly, and looked like a mass of gore and flesh, without the least resemblance to the human face."

And but a few pages later: "I laid on the blows thick and fast, until his face was nearly cut to pieces, and he laid on the ground senseless, passively receiving the tremendous blows that I dealt out to him. He might have been killed, if the men had not forced me off."

Wyman was either a tremendous closet pugilist or full of beans. Either way, in addition to his skills at fisticuffs, he would have made a fine writer of pulp fiction.

At various times in his life, Wyman tried to go straight, to back away from the many illegal aspects of the life he led. But as with most of us who tire of a new exercise regimen, Wyman always ended up slipping back into his well-worn and predictable routines, or what he called "roguery" and "tricks," his pet names for thievery and the light-fingeredness.

When scrutinizing the escapades brought about by his seemingly unquenchable desire to engage in his "tricks," doubtful readers need only regard the long litter of court cases documenting those exploits at which he was caught.

Regarding his methods, and his premeditation, Wyman is coolly matter-of-fact. "It has always been my policy, when I was obliged to conceal my plunder, to carry it to premises belonging to some other person, generally to some one whom I disliked, so that if it was discovered, it would do me some good." And it should be noted that the people he disliked also and uniformly disliked him, notably longtime, long-suffering neighbors who had plenty of reason to dislike the man.

Of all the varied goods he stole, of curious note is Wyman's penchant for filching bolts of cloth. Ever the dandy, it seems he could not resist fine weaves for use in suits of clothes that he had tailor-made. He managed to secret extraordinary amounts of yard goods in an item that he stole as a young man and that accompanied him for many years of thievery—a large cloak. Under this garment, he was able to secure many goods on a "shopping" trip: "Whenever I went out for the purpose of helping myself to other people's property, I invariably wore this as a kind of storehouse for stolen goods."

On one day alone, he admits to stealing an assortment of expensive tools from inside an unfinished house, as well as various lengths of cloth from a shop and three private homes. He says that later he heard that a large amount of cloth had been missed, but that, "at all event, they have never troubled me at all."

And that sums up another of Wyman's jerkiest traits: The man never once shows remorse for any of his victims. He is so self-absorbed that his first, last, and abiding thoughts are to steal for his own amusement. This he defines as money for fine clothes, for drink, and for amusing women.

He reached a turning point in his life when, as a young man, he bedded the unhappily married wife of a friend, made a mess of that family, then skipped town and left the woman, Welthy Loomis Chandler, waiting for him. He decamped to Boston, whereupon he continued his thieving capers at an increased rate. First he fell in with a gang of—would you believe it—thieves!

With his trademark lack of humility, Wyman proceeded to show them how true thievery was done. He claims that using his methods, they tripled their haul within hours. He soon grew bored with them and uncharacteristically decided to chuck it all and join the militia. He spent much time in the local garrison, mostly gaming and drinking and gambling, before being told that they were not taking on any new soldiers at that time. So Wyman did what any young man would do: He stole a bundle of new boots to help fund his future exploits and took to the road.

In 1808, after a long, drawn-out series of impressive adventures with friends on the road, winning and losing around the gambling tables, and imbibing much libation—Wyman enjoyed hard drink—he married his long-ago love, Welthy Loomis Chandler, back in Boston. She was a woman for whom he endured his first jail term on a charge of adultery and, not ironically, for theft. He proved to be (somewhat) faithful to her, poor thing, and they would eventually have six children together.

As he aged and faced an increase in familial demands, Wyman turned to higher-stakes pursuits such as passing counterfeit cash. His jail terms came more frequently, often in deplorable conditions. He attempted escape and, according to him, managed to make it up and out of the walls a few times, too.

In 1815 he and his family decamped to Maine, where he gave farming another go. Wonder of wonders, it still did not suit him. By 1817 he was in court in Augusta, Maine, facing a larceny conviction, for which he earned three years at the state prison in Charlestown, Massachusetts. He served but a year, which his poor wife and offspring spent in charity housing in Boston. He moved his family back to New Hampshire and soon found himself—you guessed it—stealing bolts of cloth. Apparently his age slowed his reflexes, for he was caught and once again shuttled back to prison, this time to the New Hampshire State Prison for Men in Concord.

After that jail stint, he managed to keep his nose clean, owing to both a back injury suffered in a fall on a construction job site and, presumably, the love of a devoted wife. Seth Wyman died on April 2, 1843, and while he may have written his book with the intention of it being a cautionary tale, it is obvious that Wyman was more than a wee bit proud of his past exploits as he jotted them down. Surely someone as narcissistic and misanthropic as he wasn't wholly convinced that his life's story wouldn't make for darned good reading.

Seth Wyman is a classic example of a born misanthrope, but he was so much more than that. Here was an educated man born into a loving, giving family, a man who did not know privation in his youth, a man with obvious intelligence, apparent good looks, and charm—or at least the ability to persuade. But more to the point, he was a knowing jerk and would have us believe that while he spent his life stealing from others and doing his best to avoid legal labor, he never killed anyone.

While that may be true, he also actively undertook pursuits he knew would cause harm to others emotionally, physically, financially, and socially. Yet he plundered on, smiling and whistling the entire time. His thefts surely hastened innocent victims to lives of poverty and earlier demise than they might otherwise have experienced had he not filched the tools of their trade, the food from their pantries, the clothes from their lines, the goods from their shelves.

Still, Wyman's book is a highly readable account of a life ill lived. His repeated escapades, at times presented in a rapid-fire manner, read like a laundry list of his crimes, from first to last. But the book never grows boring or redundant, mostly because Wyman always seems so darned amused at his own exploits and pleased with his numerous successes.

For all his misdeeds and misadventures, his was a common life, and any uncommon attributes it may have had we owe only to the fact that he penned his autobiography, no doubt embellishing mightily (who wouldn't, if given the chance to relive his past with no one about to contradict or cast a cocked, disapproving eye?).

One can easily imagine this pathetic criminal sitting in his cold cell in the state prison at Charlestown, Massachusetts, ink staining his aged fingers as he feverishly penned his exploits, cackling to himself.

In the end, how much to believe and how much to take with a shaker full of salt? That he lived, caused many people many hardships, fathered many children, broke many hearts, among them parents, loves, friends, spouses, and children, spent time in and out of jails and prisons, wrote a book about his life's alleged exploits, and then died, penniless and bitter, much of this is public record and thus qualifies him for jerk status. That he was seemingly beyond redemption and without real regret or remorse, qualifies him for pathetic jerk status.

Though by his own admission his life was one long series of foul deeds, it cannot be denied that Seth Wyman was a born raconteur.

Even if but half of the book is true, the man was a societal leech and had, by his own account, "a life which has been worse than useless." But he was also entertaining as all get-out.

And now that his book is in the public domain, free for the reading, it's not something that can be stolen from a shelf. One has to wonder what Wyman would think of that.

## CHAPTER 17

# Louis H. F. Wagner:
## *The Smuttynose Killer*

Six miles from the coast of New Hampshire, Smuttynose Island—so named because when the tide's out, the seaweed-covered rock at one end resembles a long snout—is nonetheless part of the state of Maine. Despite this, the long, sod-covered isle is more coveted by New Hampshirites than Mainers, as the state border runs right to the island.

The collection of islands in the shoals has long been home to fishermen and, beginning in the latter half of the nineteenth century, summercators and tourists. On Appledore Island, poetess Celia Thaxter's family built a grand and famous inn, the Appledore House, in hopes of accommodating the increasing numbers of tourists interested in visiting the handsome handful of islands.

Smuttynose, third largest of the Isles of Shoals, behind Appledore and Star Islands, is particularly picturesque and undeserving of its top claim to fame as the setting of one of New England's most horrific murders. The incident nonetheless proves that willful villainy exists in the world, and never was it more in evidence than just past midnight, in the earliest hours of March 6, 1873.

Louis H. F. Wagner had grown tired of rowing, bone numbingly tired. But he still had miles to go and, true to traits of his stalwart Prussian ancestry, he refused to give in to mere physical exhaustion. Not when such a prize was so close and so easily plucked.

He leaned forward, pulled long and hard at the oars, doubling his efforts. He rowed with the tide, a good thing, as the twelve miles from Portsmouth would be impossible otherwise. And as he rowed, he busied his mind with thoughts of what he would do with the $600 he would soon possess. Why, in America, such an amount could carry a man far, set him up in business, and well away from

*Maren Hontvet (and her little dog, Ringe) barely survived*
*Louis Wagner's Smuttynose killing spree.*

those who would no doubt seek to punish him for what he was about to do.

But such an opportunity might not present itself to him again for a long time, and he did not have the time or patience to let this chance pass him by. Ivan Christensen and John Hontvet would be in Portsmouth awaiting their bait, then setting the trawl, thousands of hooks' worth for the little schooner. He knew this much, for he had been in Portsmouth just a few hours before, chatting with the men, his friends.

As he worked the long-handled oars, slicing and pulling, slicing and pulling, he recalled how he had seen them at the docks in Portsmouth, the fishing partners from Smuttynose. And that is how he knew that the women, and their cash savings, hoarded as those Norwegians do, were back at Smuttynose, in the little cottage. Unprotected.

He had wondered then as he helped tie up their schooner. Would the men be returning to the island that night? When? As he helped them sell their catch at the dock, he had asked three times, as it turned out. And three times the patient Norwegians had explained that their bait was late, but they would head back to their home in all haste that night, as soon as they finished.

Had fishing been good for them this winter? Wagner had asked his friends as pleasantly as he could. Again he was rewarded with information that made clear to him that he must put into action his plan, and on that very night. It was a plan he had been working on for some time.

Yes, John had said. Fishing had been good—he'd managed to save roughly $600, with which they hoped to buy a schooner. And then the fools had asked him to help them bait their trawl. Wagner had almost laughed at them. Did they not realize he had no intention of staying that night in Portsmouth? When those fools were playing with their beloved bait, he would be at their house on Smuttynose, relieving them of their saved money.

If it had been ordained from on high, Wagner could not have planned it any better. Everything was working out in his favor. The moon offered just enough light for him to steer by, but not enough for prying eyes from ashore to see him. The tide was with him, and the air, surprisingly comfortable for an early spring night, was not filled with the harsh, biting winds so often found on the coast.

And David Burke, that lout, had left a fine dory unattended, perfect for such a long row. Wagner made his way out the Piscataqua River's mouth, rowed hard toward the open sea, and hove into view of the lighthouses there, before continuing on.

And then he was within sight of Appledore Island, so close and familiar, even in the near dark, its silent hump rising into the skyline before him. Onward he worked the oars, the locks keeping a steady rhythm with his efforts, measuring the hard pace he set for himself. Soon he was within yards of Smuttynose itself.

He quickly beached the pilfered craft, stole ashore, and wound his way up to the little cluster of buildings, knowing from experience, having been a guest in their home the previous summer, just where the house would be. No light shone from inside; he hadn't expected anyone would be awake at this hour, and he was pleased to see that was the case.

The door latch pleased him further—it was unlocked from the inside. After all, why would three women alone on an island consider they were in any danger? They were probably expecting their men to arrive late.

Quickly Wagner closed the door and bent his tall body, lest he be seen in the dim light. But someone did sense him there—it was Karen. She was not supposed to be there and must be visiting from her place of employ at Thaxter's at Appledore. "John?"

Before she could say more, and in all probability alert the others, Wagner hefted a stout wooden chair and drove it hard at her, into her face. But it was so dark in the house he could only aim where he hoped it would do the most damage and shut her up quickly.

From the other room he heard Maren shout. In reply, Karen screamed, "John is killing me!" So, she thought Louis was her brother-in-law—all the better.

From the adjoining room he heard Maren's voice in their native tongue. Wagner reached over and slid a stick of wood into the door handle, jamming her inside. There would be time to deal with her once he had dealt with this one. And then there was the other one in there with Maren, Ivan's young wife, Anethe, howling like a child, wondering what was happening, why was their beloved John doing this? Good, good, let them continue to think it was John. Wagner stuck to the shadows and kept his mouth shut.

He needed to find the money, $600 that would be his soon. Then he would get in that little boat and row away, and none would be the wiser.

But the women were not making it easy for him, damn them. He paused at the door to the shut room—in there were Maren and pretty Anethe. He heard them shout to the battered Karen, heard their hurried whisperings, heard Maren's damnable little dog, Ringe, barking, barking, barking. Louis thought of slipping free the stick, but wait . . . was that the window sliding open? Yes! The women were trying to make an escape. He could not let them get away.

Louis kicked at the half-shut front door of the house and thundered outside, snatching up the broken-handled axe they kept by the back door to chip ice from the well water. As he rounded the corner of the house he saw the small, pretty Anethe there before him in her nightshirt, Maren inside the window, shouting to her to run, run!

But she did not, and as Louis drew closer, his breath pluming into the chill night air, Anethe shouted, "Louis, Louis, Louis!" She ruined it for him—it would all be her fault for recognizing him. She deserved this. . . .

He set upon the girl with a grunt. The axe seemed to drive into her head of its own accord. He delivered several blows to stifle her whimpering, but the first, he was sure, had done the trick. Her head had been cleaved. For a moment, Louis stood over the spattered body on the ground at his feet, the blood a spreading shadow on the ground. It soon seeped under his boots. He breathed hard and wiped at his face with the back of one hand.

From inside the room he heard the barking dog, the inside door rattle, then open. He grunted, turned back to the front door and saw that Karen was gone from where he had hit her with the chair. The bedroom door had been closed again and the dog still barked inside. Louis lunged for it, rattled it in its frame. From inside he heard the frantic screams of Maren, begging her older sister, Karen, to get up, to come with her.

Louis smiled then, a toothy look with his lips drawn back as if he were about to bite an apple. He drove a foot at the door and it slammed inward, shoving the prone form of the mortally wounded Karen out of the way. There was Maren by the window! He mustn't let her get away!

Ringe, the dog, continued his barking. Louis snatched up a leaning chair beside the door and hurled it at Maren even as he advanced, the axe in his other hand. He swung it high, the head glancing off the ceiling, and then brought it down with great force. It lodged in the windowsill just as Maren slipped through, carrying Ringe. One stride closer and he would have had her!

He roved the island, searching each and every abandoned hut and house and fish shed for that devil woman. She had seen him, had seen what he had done, but try as he might, he could not find her. It seemed forever that he searched, stopping now and again to listen for a sign of the dog. Surely its yipping would give it away. He could not see what direction she had taken in the hard-packed snow. But she could not have gotten far on foot—it was an island, after all, and she was barefoot and ill-clothed, too.

As he searched he felt an increasing hot urgency to get back to the mainland, to set the little borrowed craft adrift, and flee in a veil of intended innocence, maybe to Boston . . . and then? Anywhere far away.

He knew he could not last well nor long enough at the oars, not with the sustained effort that they would require of him. So he returned to the little house, found the wash basin and cloth, and outside at the well he attempted to clean himself. Finally, frustrated at so much blood already dried on his hands, on his face, and staining his clothes, with a snarl, Louis threw the basin and bloodied washcloth down the well. He dragged the stiffening dead woman, Anethe, into the house, lest early daylight reveal her too soon to whoever might happen along. He reasoned that every minute gained would be worthwhile.

He found a plate, fork, and knife, and set to the task of supping quickly of the food that Maren and Anethe had no doubt prepared for their husbands, expecting them to return that night. He had also managed to make quick tea with help of the still-warm kettle.

Lastly, he ransacked the house and found nothing but fifteen dollars, damn their tight Norwegian purse strings!

Finally he made his way back to the boat and shoved off into the chill tide. As he rowed, unbidden memories came to him of the many nights he'd spent under the very roof of those women and men just the preceding summer. They were kind—too kind at times. Always obliging, offering a hand when one was scarcely needed, and willingly sharing their food, their conversation, their genuine friendship. But none of these things, though they occurred to him, did much to alter how he felt about what he had just done.

A quick glimpse of the spray-crusted oar, a long, stiff thing caked with frozen sea spume, suddenly reminded him of the body of Anethe. He had stared at the beautiful creature as she lay unmoving on the kitchen floor. But now, as he pulled at the oars toward Portsmouth, he knew he had the strength he needed to get there. If he had only found that damnable Maren and the money!

To say that Jorge Ingebertsen, on nearby Appledore Island, was shocked when he rowed over to Smuttynose after seeing Maren shouting and waving to him would be a gross understatement. She had always been a happy, cheerful woman, a wonderful neighbor to him and his wife and children, along with her husband, John. And life had only gotten better for them all when Maren's relations from Norway had come to live and work with them.

First, her sister, Karen, who worked for the Thaxters at their inn on Appledore, then her brother Ivan and his new bride, the beautiful Anethe. Such lovely people. But now here was Maren, still in her nightclothes, barefoot and barely able to stay upright on bloodied, frozen feet. Most shocking of all were her bruised face and her wild eyes, frantic like a hunted animal's.

"Maren, what has happened? Who did this to you?"

"Louis!"

As Ingebertsen rowed her back to his place, he tried to get more information out of her, but could only get the name Louis, that cursed Wagner—it had to be him. But just what had he done? Something bad had happened, that much was certain. But as to the extent of it, he could not be certain. Surely Maren's raving was confused and could not be true.

Ingebertsen left her with the Thaxters and fetched armed men. But once they made their way to Smuttynose, to the Hontvet's house, they saw for themselves that Maren had told the truth, and within seconds they came to understand more of what had happened on the island the night before. The bloody scene was almost more than the men could bear, more horrific than any war's battle they might have encountered.

Later, they found out the entire story from Maren, who sat in bed at the Thaxters' house. She had made it through the window, she'd said, before the axe narrowly missed her leg as she leapt free of the sill. On her way out she had managed to grab a skirt and her dog, Ringe. She had been tempted to slide under one of the nearby fish sheds, but she suspected the dog would give her away and attract the murderous Louis.

No, she told herself, she had to run, to get as far away as she could. But where to hide? She had finally scrambled down to the water's edge and wedged herself as far as she was able into a cleft in the rocks. It was there she had waited out the night, huddled barefoot and barely clothed, and clutching her little dog, Ringe, tight for warmth. She knew she had to keep the dog silent, hardly daring to breathe when all she really wanted to do was scream.

Maren did not emerge from her rocky hide until daybreak, not knowing if Louis Wagner had left the island or if he were still stalking her, the broken axe clutched tight in his big hand, the blood of Karen and Anethe spattered all over him and dripping from the axe head.

Men left to fetch more men, more guns, to scour the nearby islands to look for Louis Wagner. They all knew of him, though not many cared for the sullen Prussian, not many trusted him. But if Maren had said it was he who had done this, then it was he, for she would have no reason to lie to them. The Norwegian men were still gone, their fishing having kept them away for the night, but they all knew the men would surely be home soon.

Other island men roved Smuttynose, their eyes drawn to the most blatant and hideous of clues. They followed a man's bloody boot prints in the snow, from the house, across the raw terrain to other empty houses, to the outbuildings and fish sheds, all around them, the man had searched as they now searched for him. It was evident that that bloody-booted man had been searching for Maren. So where was he now?

A search of the surrounding islands was thorough but turned up no Louis Wagner. Officials from the mainland were sent for. And in the meantime, the white sails of John Hontvet's fishing vessel could be seen gliding into view. From shore, the men beckoned them to dock at Appledore. They had to prepare them somehow, had to tell them what they would find on their home island of Smuttynose.

And so the men were told, and they stole to the island, rowing the gut in haste. Surely this was a mistake. Surely this was a joke! Ivan lurched up the shore, followed closely by John, who had learned that his own wife, Maren, had been spared whatever horrors they were told they would soon find. But nothing the other men said could prepare them for this. Nothing.

Ivan saw his young wife, Anethe, so lovely and vibrant a creature. He idolized, worshipped, and cared for her as though she were a delicate bird. But seeing her stretched out on the kitchen floor, her long blonde hair, once like sunlight, now matted to her head, pasted in blood where that fiend had split her skull wide open. Blood had spattered everywhere outside and puddled inside, sprayed about the walls, the floor, the furniture. . . .

And close by, Karen, sister to Maren and Ivan, now a bloodied, battered thing. But why? What could Louis Wagner have hoped to gain? They looked later and found that he had missed the thing it seemed he had most wanted—their saved money, folded and hidden beneath clothes in a drawer, a drawer he had ransacked with too much haste.

The next day, Louis Wagner was found in Boston. He had made it increasingly easy for the police, and eventually for prosecutors, to implicate him. Once he returned early that morning to the mainland, he had acted as one tortured by a conscience laden with guilt over bad deeds done. He had been seen pulling the little borrowed dory ashore, had been seen repeatedly trying to set it adrift again, only to have the craft come back time and again as the tide worked against him.

He had finally returned to the Portsmouth rooming house he'd been staying at, where he changed his clothes. He'd acted nervous as he told the other boarders and his landlady that he'd done something "very bad" and that he would be going away, never to see them again. Then he left.

Wagner had made his way to Boston on the train, where he used the paltry amount of money he had killed for—less than twenty dollars—to get a haircut and beard trim and buy a new suit of clothes (he discarded his old clothes there at the suit shop), and he told someone at a hotel that he'd killed two fishermen. In a shoe store, he pointed at merchandise and told the proprietor that he'd "seen a woman lay as still as that shoe there." And so it would seem guilt and the creep of madness layered in his mind like wet, wool blankets, suffocating and cloying him until he might burst.

But he did not burst. He merely stayed in Boston. Why didn't Louis Wagner move on? Surely he wasn't so obtuse as to think he would not be tracked down? That Maren had seen him do the most foul things a person can do and would not tell? Had he hoped that she might have somehow died in the night?

When the law finally caught up with Wagner in Boston the evening of the day following the murders, one wonders if the foul murderer felt relief. If he did, it was short-lived, because thousands of incensed citizens greeted his armed escort at Portsmouth, shouting harsh threats and calling for his lynching. Rocks and bricks were hurled, and several law enforcement officials were injured.

And it didn't end there: The next day hundreds of residents of the Shoals region stormed the jailhouse with lynching on their mind. But Wagner was too well guarded and the crowd's vigilante fervor abated enough that, though still angered, they faltered and dispersed.

Since it had been determined that the crime took place under Maine's jurisdiction, as Smuttynose lay in the York County town of Kittery, Wagner was moved first to South Berwick, then to the newly built prison at the county seat of Alfred, Maine, for trial. Incredibly, while there Louis picked the lock on his cell, and, rigging a dummy in his cot, he and two other inmates escaped.

He made his way to Farmington, New Hampshire, where he was found less than two weeks later. This time Maine police kept him under closer scrutiny. Given the fact that the heinous crime had received much national press attention, the escape proved a mighty embarrassment for them.

During the highly publicized trial, Wagner proclaimed his innocence loudly and often. Despite this, the evidence against him was ample, and included a button found in his pocket that had been in Karen's possession. She had intended the next day to try to find a mate for it on a shopping trip in Portsmouth. He also left numerous fingerprints and bootprints all over the victims' house, and bloody handprints on the kettle, on silverware where he had eaten a meal after he'd done the grisly deed.

The dory he stole had suffered noticeable wear on the oarlocks, especially since the owner swore they were nearly new before Wagner had appropriated the craft. He had been seen by many people early that morning walking to Portsmouth, having left the dory in New Castle, presumably to avoid drawing attention to it. Witnesses recall that he looked unkempt.

At his boardinghouse he had changed his shirt and stuffed his old, bloodied shirt in the outhouse. This was later found, and though he said the blood was fish guts, forensic medicine at the time was advanced enough to discern that it was not fish but human blood on the shirt. Even the bloody bootprints on the island were matched to Wagner's boots.

Though it had no bearing in the trial, in 1904, when the building in which he'd roomed was being redone, workmen found a dagger hidden beneath the floorboards in the room in which he'd lived.

During the trial, the most damning evidence of all came not from Maren Hontvet's heartbreaking testimony, but from Wagner himself. He fabricated an involved story of that night's events, none of the facts of which could be substantiated in any way.

He claimed to have helped a fisherman bait his trawls though could not recall the man's name. He claimed to have been drinking at a bar in Portsmouth but could not recall the name of the establishment. He even said he had bedded down for the night in the room next to the Hontvets' at a rooming house, but no evidence was found to support this. His own landlady swore under oath that she had not seen him return to her boardinghouse that night. Lastly he claimed he had only been curious—repeatedly—about the Hontvet women because he had promised to help transport a woman named Johanna to the islands. No woman by this name was ever found.

It took the jury less than an hour—fifty-five minutes—to find Louis H. F. Wagner guilty of murder in the first degree. He was sentenced to hang by the neck until dead. And on June 25, 1875, he did—as one half of a double hanging. Wagner maintained his innocence to the very end. He was so persuasive that on the day of his hanging, the warden at Thomaston prison said he still believed Wagner was innocent.

Believe it or not, Louis Wagner swung right next to another Maine axe murderer with whom he shared the scaffold. The other man, John Gordon, aka the Thorndike Killer, had, also in 1873 and also with an axe, murdered his brother, his sister-in-law, and their baby daughter, all while they slept. He also attacked his nephew with the axe, but though injured, the boy lived. Gordon then tried to burn the house down to cover his foul deed. And all because of a dispute over the inheritance of the Thorndike farm.

It is difficult to overestimate the nationwide notorious and sensational nature of Wagner's trial. Many news outlets called it the trial of the century. Much of this owed to the horrific nature of the crimes, especially as they were perpetrated against women and in such a heinous manner. But it was also mighty intriguing that Wagner insisted on his innocence throughout the proceedings, from his arrest, trial, and conviction on through his escape, capture, imprisonment, and execution at Thomaston, Maine.

The Smuttynose murder house would be hacked and hewn apart, piece by piece, over the coming months and years by morbid visitors seeking prizes, claiming pieces of the crime, knowing no shame, and thrilling at their secret pilfered bits. The house no longer stands, having burned in 1885.

Though numerous artists, writers, painters, and others who have been inspired by the beauty of the Isles of Shoals have revered them in song, story, poem, and painting, their artistic efforts are still largely outshone by the Smuttynose murders, which have generated their own long list of works of art, film, books, stories, and songs.

## CHAPTER 18

# Lt. Bennett Young & His Confederate Cohorts: *Bank-Robbing Rebel Raiders*

Unthinkable! Inconceivable! Preposterous! And yet, on October 19, 1864, there really was a Confederate raid on little ol' St. Albans, Vermont, a small town that sits close to the border with Canada, far, far north of where the war's primary activities took place. Just how did this come about? History lays the blame at the feet of one bold man, Lt. Bennett H. Young of the Confederate States Army.

Just twenty-one at the time of the incident, Bennett Young was understandably idealistic and filled with passion for the Confederate cause, a cause that had begun to fray at the edges. The Confederate States Army (CSA) desperately needed money, and Lieutenant Young was in on a plan, organized by Confederate agent George Sanders, that he felt confident, should he pull it off, would net the CSA a pile of much-needed currency. And better yet, it was money that belonged to the hated Union. It was also hoped that the plan would distract and draw Union troops from battles in the South in an effort to protect its northern border.

It would be a mighty triple blow. The downside? The plan looked unlikely to succeed from any angle. But brash Lieutenant Young was nothing if not persuasive. And besides, reasoned his superiors, what did they really have to lose?

Bennett Henderson Young was the third son of Robert and Josephine (Henderson) Young, both devout Presbyterians sporting long Southern lineage. Born in Nicholasville, Jessamine County, Kentucky, on May 25, 1843, Bennett received his childhood schooling at Bethel Academy and, in 1861, entered Centre College, in

*Though revered later in life as a true Southern gentleman, years before, Lt. Bennett Young and his Confederate Army cohorts terrorized a northern Vermont town, robbing banks, killing a civilian, and trying to burn the burg.*

COURTESY LIBRARY OF CONGRESS

Danville, Kentucky. By the time he reached eighteen in 1862, Young, along with so many incensed young Southern men his age, enlisted in the Confederate army. He was placed in Company B, 8th Kentucky Cavalry, as a private, commanded by Capt. William Lewis, and under Col. Leroy S. Clarke.

In 1863, this company eventually came under the command of Maj. Gen. John Hunt Morgan and was present during Morgan's failed but famed raid on Ohio. It was there, on July 26, 1863, during the Battle of Salineville, that Morgan was forced to surrender to Northern troops. The battle was notable in that it was the northernmost engagement of the Civil War, a point not quickly forgotten by Young.

And he would have plenty of time to ruminate on it, because Bennett Young, along with his fellow Confederate soldiers, was captured at Columbiana, Saline County, Ohio. They became prisoners of war and were briefly incarcerated at Camp Chase, Columbus, Ohio. Shortly thereafter, Young and others were moved to Camp Douglas, near Chicago, Illinois. He attempted escape but failed and spent the next thirty days in an underground cell as punishment.

In January 1864, he attempted to escape a second time and succeeded. Young fled north to Canada, where he found it was too late in the season to hop aboard a boat heading down the St. Lawrence River. Not one to squander his time, and ever a man eager for education, Young stayed in Canada and enrolled at the University of Toronto until April. Then he took command of his fellow escaped Confederate prisoners, and they found passage aboard the first boat heading south.

The returning sons of the South soon found themselves coursing along the southeastern US coast, drawing ever closer to kith and kin. But they found their homecoming to be a battle zone. Under fire, their vessel headed through the blockade at the port of Wilmington, North Carolina. The battle turned against them, the situation appeared dire, crew members were killed, and by many accounts, it was the cool head of Bennett Young that saved the day. Safely back in Confederate territory, Young was rewarded by being made a first lieutenant in the CSA.

Lieutenant Young was sent back to Canada and participated in a number of undercover missions on the Confederacy's behalf. He even returned to Chicago to the very prison camp in which he had been held—Camp Douglas—in an effort to liberate the rebel soldiers being held there. Unbeknownst to Lieutenant Young, he had a traitor in his midst, and the plot was foiled. He helped hatch a second plan to liberate Camp Chase, in Columbus, Ohio, another facility in which he had been incarcerated. That plan also failed to come to fruition. Most men would be beaten down by such a series of setbacks, but Lt. Bennett H. Young was not like most other men. He headed back to Canada to reconnoiter.

Why not try to divert Union attention to its northern border with Canada, a country that wished to remain neutral in the fight? Why not use Canada to help the Confederacy? Why not pillage and burn key US towns along the border, rob them of their wealth, and use the money to help fund the CSA effort? And that is precisely what the CSA planned to do.

By October 19, 1864, it had taken the twenty-one Confederate soldiers, all former prisoners of war, nine days to drift down from Canada in groups of two and three, but they all finally assembled in the placid little northern Vermont town of St. Albans, a mere fifteen miles below the Canadian border. The amiable, clean-cut young strangers had been telling locals for the previous week that they were there on a sporting vacation from Saint-Jean, Quebec. At 3 p.m., on October 19, the men spread throughout the bustling little burg of St. Albans.

Half of the newcomers corralled awestruck residents onto the town common while the rest of the invaders went about stealing horses. Lt. Bennett Young then climbed the steps of a hotel and shouted, "This city is now in the possession of the Confederate States of America!"

The absurdity of the situation almost threatened to override the quiet autumn day. But the raiders had other plans. They entered the town's three banks in separate groups. At each bank they forced the employees and customers at gunpoint to repeat an oath to the Confederacy: "I swear allegiance to Jeff Davis and the Confederate States of America."

At one bank, the manager, either too slow to comprehend the potential danger of the bizarre situation, or in an effort to protect his bank from looting, defied the raiders' orders. One of the gun-toting young men strode to him, barked "damn Yankee dog!" and clouted the banker above his ear with the butt of a pistol. The vicious head wound convinced the others in the bank to acquiesce to the frantic raiders' demands. A few of the other reticent bankers were dealt with in a similar fashion as they were forced to lie facedown on the floor while the graybacks looted the banks' vaults.

In the huddled mass of folk on the town common, one local tried to pitch a raider from his mount. But in the ensuing scuffle, the daring villager was shot dead (by some accounts accidentally) by the still-mounted Confederate raider. Random gunshots, angry shouts, and the cries of roughly treated residents echoed through the small town and convinced the villagers they were indeed in the midst of a town-wide rebel attack!

Soon, the howling Confederates, brandishing their pistols, had finished robbing the banks of roughly $200,000. The raiders milled about the throngs of village residents, their horses stomping and churning the green grass and dropped leaves. The rebs leveled their pistols at the men who dared to look them in the eye and curse them for their so-called act of war. Most of the townsmen, for their part, did their best to place themselves between the agitated, shouting riders and the women and children of the town, many of the latter crying in fear and confusion.

Finally the raiders' leader, Lieutenant Young, rode among his men, doing his best to ignore the angered Vermonters. His bellowed shouts of victory and of Confederate supremacy were met with cheers by his men and shouts of disbelief and rage by the locals.

The raiders' frenzy of excitement was so great they dropped sacks of cash and nearly ran one another down in the street. Despite their nervous confusion in attempting to flee the town, they rode hard down Main Street and northward, Lieutenant Young repeating barked orders to burn the entire town to the ground.

Each man had been outfitted with bottles of the incendiary, volatile liquid called "Greek fire," and Young ordered his men to throw the bottles hard at each building as they raced through the small town's streets, bent on razing the place to the ground.

Even as they galloped through, the residents ran to their homes for weapons, to retrieve horses, to send for the doctor, and to warn others nearby that the Confederate army, as incredible as it seemed, had invaded Vermont! They faced a grim situation, fearing that at any moment waves of graybacks might descend on St. Albans and kill them all. The raiders' departure offered some solace to the citizens of St. Albans, a number of whom did their best to follow the northward-fleeing thieves, but the raiders had too much of a head start on them.

For the rebels, setting the entire damn Yankee town alight was to be a most fitting tribute to their beloved Confederacy. But in this effort, they were thwarted. Bottle after bottle of their precious liquid weapons were hurled at the houses, businesses, barns, and stables as they thundered through the town. And while the bottles exploded, and flames licked at the wood, that was all they did. The promise of those early, new conflagrations guttered and fizzled, barely causing smoke.

Out of all the brutal carnage they could have caused, only one small woodshed succumbed to the disappointing flames. Hardly the inferno of their dreams, hardly the smoking wreck into which they had wished to turn this Northern town, much the same as the Union army had done to towns and cities throughout the South.

Another of their intended targets had been the mansion of St. Albans resident and then Vermont governor J. Gregory Smith, who was away at the time of the raid, attending to state affairs at the capital city of Montpelier. A neighbor ran to tell Mrs. Smith that the town had been overrun by rebels and that they were headed her way. The raiders, however, perhaps sensing a need for urgency, skipped savaging that particular prize.

Not knowing the rebels' plans, the governor's wife shuttered the windows, locked the doors, and, standing defiantly before the front door, defended their home with an unloaded pistol, the only weapon she could find. Presently she heard a horse approaching at a hard gallop and steeled herself for some sort of standoff. It proved to be her brother-in-law, who'd been home on leave from his duties under Brigadier General Custer. He made sure all was secure, then departed to spread the word of the raid. Within hours, Union soldiers had been dispatched to defend the governor's home.

The twenty-one Confederates, led by Young, made it to Canada, where fourteen were captured and arrested. The United States demanded that the men be extradited. But Canada, in its attempt to remain neutral and even-handed, decided that the raid had been an act of war, and since Canada was neutral on the matter of the war and wished to remain so, the Canadian powers that be felt they had no choice but to free the fourteen. The captured raiders were in possession of $86,000, which Canada confiscated and returned to the town of St. Albans.

What of the other men? They remained at large, along with their portions of the loot. One of them, William Travis, disguised himself as a girl and ventured south, with his money, all the way back to Confederate territory.

Were New Englanders so removed from the events of the seemingly never-ending war that they would fail to react strongly to such a bold affront? As it happens, they were not. In a war in which 3,000,000 men fought, and 620,000 men (2 percent of the US population) died, the three northern New England states lost tremendous numbers of young men. In a single week of fighting in May 1864, a Vermont brigade lost 1,645 of its 2,100 men fighting in the Battle of the Wilderness, in Virginia. Of the 33,947 New Hampshire men who served in the Union army, 4,882 died. And an appalling record was set by the 1st Maine Heavy Artillery, which lost 635 of its 900 men in the first seven minutes of fighting at Petersburg, Virginia, on June 18, 1864.

These were mighty blows to such small states with relatively low populations made up of largely rural, farming folk with not a lot to offer the cause—assuming they even agreed with it. Most were more concerned with putting enough food by and staying solvent enough to not lose their homes. In that respect, they were not much different than their Southern counterparts, average hardworking families south of the Mason-Dixon line, most of whom owned no slaves.

During the war, Bennett Young was made a general of the Confederate States Army, but afterward he was denied amnesty by President Andrew Johnson and spent several years in exile. But he was not idle. Young headed to Ireland and Scotland, where he spent his time pursuing his collegiate studies, including law, until

1868, when he was allowed to return to the United States. He made his way back to his beloved Kentucky and over the course of a busy, rich life, rose to prominence as one of the most successful and respected attorneys in the Louisville region.

In 1911, on a visit to Montreal, Young met with a group of representatives from St. Albans and shared a cordial tea at the Ritz-Carlton Hotel. The town commemorated the raid on its fiftieth anniversary in 1914, with a plaque on the building that had been the First County Bank during the raid. Though at the time Lieutenant Young's raid had terrorized the residents of the tiny border town, St. Albans has since grown oddly proud of the fact that the northernmost action of the Civil War took place there.

To Young's credit, it is said that in his later years he refused to gamble, smoke, drink, or swear in the presence of a woman. He also founded Louisville's first orphanage for blacks, as well as a school for the blind, and often engaged in pro bono work for those who could not afford legal counsel.

Young died on February 23, 1919, at the age of seventy-six, but he is far from forgotten—way down South, and far to the North.

The raid on St. Albans, this northernmost action of the Civil War, aka the War between the States (which many Southerners still often refer to as the War of Northern Aggression) was looked upon by many Southerners as a bold and heroic effort by a man worthy of admiration. Farther north, however, the act was regarded as shameful and cowardly. Which just goes to prove that one man's hero is another man's . . . jerk? Nowhere is that sentiment bound to creep up more than in discussion of warfare.

The infamous raid on St. Albans was more than a mere act of war. It was a desperate attempt by a desperate entity to loot money from its enemy. It was also an effort to bring the war to Northern soil in an attempt to divert Union troops from a long-term, concentrated assault under which the CSA was withering. But using the war to justify such behavior doesn't cleanse the perpetrators of their guilt of committing terrorist activities on private citizens. St. Albans, Vermont, was no Union stronghold. It was a small town with three banks close by a convenient escape route. And that's why the Confederacy chose it as a target—easy pickings for thievery.

And yet, in light of the impressive individual Bennett Young became, it is difficult to cast him in a wholly disparaging light, until one considers that the residents of quiet St. Albans that October day in 1864 surely felt convinced their deaths might be mere moments away.

## CHAPTER 19

# Emeline Meaker & Mary Rogers:
## *The Lady Killers*

W ho says women can't be jerks? Just because women are often kinder in general than men, just because they are often more soft spoken and less prone to violence than men, just because . . . okay, you get the idea. But there are exceptions to every rule. And the Green Mountain State was home to a pair of exceptional exceptions—doozies in the personages of Emeline Meaker and Mary Rogers. But what did these two fiends do to earn such dubious distinctions?

Rarely has the world been subjected to such an unsavory and repugnant creature as Emeline Meaker. The unpleasant woman holds the distinction of being the first woman legally executed in Vermont. And for good reason, as we will soon learn.

What could have been going on in Almon Meaker's mind that cold evening of April 23, 1880, as he maneuvered the rented buggy along the Little River road away from Waterbury, Vermont, in the dark night hours? Nothing unusual in such a pursuit—unless one considers Almon's fellow passengers.

One was his mother, Emeline Meaker, a stout, stone-deaf, overbearing personage prone to histrionics and who cowed and bullied everyone who came near her. And the other passenger? None other than Almon's recently deceased nine-year-old aunt, his father's half sister Alice.

How recently deceased? Little Alice had violently gagged, convulsed, and spasmed her way into the grim reaper's bony embrace just minutes before, held tight and with a fat hand clamped tight over her mouth by the brute of a woman married to her older brother, the very woman hired by the state to take in the nine-year-old half sister to her husband.

*In 1883, Emeline Meaker, deaf bullying tyrant, swung for her foul crime of murdering a nine-year-old girl, making her the first woman legally executed in Vermont.*

Alice Meaker's young life, along with that of her brother Hilie, began poorly and never got better.

On April 23, 1880, Emeline Meaker had reached the end of her rope. She could take no more of the nine-year-old girl entrusted to her care by the state of Vermont. In truth, her dissatisfaction had begun before the girl ever arrived at their house. But only in recent weeks had she worked on the emotions of her weak-kneed son, Almon, demanding that he drive young Alice far away into the wilderness, preferably to a mountaintop, and leave her to starve there. To his credit, Almon refused. Unfortunately he would not continue to be so resistant to her demands.

Each time his mother beseeched the weak-willed and weaker-minded nineteen-year-old young man, his resolve crumbled a bit more, until he finally agreed to help his own mother kill the girl. Almon was as close to a dolt as a functioning person can become and proved to be the perfect dupe for his mother. On this evening, he would fast approach the end of a lifelong habit of being puppeteered by her.

Emeline sent Almon to town, downtown Waterbury, to purchase a few butter plates, and said that he might also pick up a smidge of strychnine at the chemist's, as they had been having trouble with rats. She also requested that, while in town, Almon rent a buggy and horse team.

When Almon arrived back home, dark descended as he parked the horses and buggy behind the barn.

When her husband finally went to bed, Emeline stole into the girl's room and made Alice get dressed. She told her they were going for a ride and then stuffed her through the window. One has to think that the poor girl, forever being beaten and whipped by the big deaf brute of a woman, must surely have suspected something was amiss, perhaps that her overbearing guardian had gone a bit further off the beam. But they made it out of the house and met Almon and the team at the lane. From there the trio proceeded out of town toward Stowe.

They traveled for some miles when Almon halted the rig atop a hill. On his mother's instruction, he mixed the strychnine in sugared water. Emeline had planned far enough in advance that she brought the girl's favorite cup, a little china cup given to Alice by her estranged mother. It read "Remember me" on the side.

While the horse's breath plumed into the cool early spring air, the dastardly pair made the girl drink the sweet liquid and then proceeded on their way. Within twenty minutes, the small, thin girl began coughing, then convulsing, gagging, and screaming as the poison began to work itself into her system. In her thrashing agony, the girl repeatedly screamed, "Mother! Mother! Mother!" as they passed near by a house owned by Mrs. Linn Foster, who heard the girl's screams.

Alice's shouts were soon stoppered by the beefy hand of Emeline clamped over her shrieking mouth. Within minutes the girl was a limp, dead thing in the virago's hands. The grim-faced pair rode on for a few more minutes, and at Emeline's instruction Almon pulled the wagon over beside a swamp. He dragged the dead girl into the bog, pulled her cloak up over her head, and buried her in a hole in the muck under a few inches of frigid water. Then he piled branches and loose debris on top of the spot. The girl's corpse would reside there for three days.

It took neighbors a day to begin to question the absence of little sad-faced Alice, who had been the object of much of Emeline's daily screaming and rage-filled tirades for so long. Flimsy excuses given by both Almon and his mother differed and seemed so implausible—"The girl has run away," said Emeline, "but don't bother to chase her down"—that neighbors finally contacted the local law, Sheriff Atherton.

One wonders why none of these pious neighbors, having witnessed the constant physical beatings and verbal abuse given the girl by Emeline for the previous several years, had ever lifted a finger to help the girl before then. Most likely it had been fear of the woman and fear of what might be thought of them should they interfere in another person's business. Even, apparently, if that other person was a bully crushing the soul out of a helpless little girl.

The clueless Horace Meaker, husband of Emeline and father to Almon, told the nosey neighbors that the girl had "come up missing" in the night. As far as he knew, this was indeed the truth. This was hardly sufficient excuse. When Sunday rolled around, more neighbors became incensed, convinced as much by Emeline's cool responses that they wouldn't spend any time or a single cent in tracking down the girl, and that if she wanted to go off, then leave her to it.

Eventually, after hearing his fill of flimsy stories from the boy and his mother, Sheriff Atherton wore down weak-willed Almon, who confessed that he and his mother had committed a most heinous deed. The sheriff drove a two-seater buggy out of town as Almon pointed the way. Within an hour or so, they arrived at the swamp. The sheriff bade the simp of a boy to tell him where they'd buried the girl.

When he reached the sad spot, the sheriff dragged away the piled debris, then drove a hand down and groped about in the foul, frigid ooze. Soon he felt that which until that very moment he had hoped he'd not find. It was the little girl's thin arm. He tugged gently but firmly, as the muck was not willing to yield its prize easily.

The lifeless girl's body finally emerged from the bog, dripping and cold. The sheriff carried the girl back to the buggy and made Almon hold her the entire trip back to the Meaker household. At first Almon balked, telling how his arms were too tired to hold the girl. The sheriff persisted, and the boy soon clasped the girl tight, leaned his head on hers, and soon was debilitated into a sobbing mess the entire trip back.

As word spread of the verification of this most foul of deeds, neighbors crowded around the Meaker home, threatening vigilante justice. The police quickly removed Almon and his mother and charged them with the murder of little Alice. Emeline proved an unruly prisoner, proclaiming her innocence. Almon never claimed his innocence, but he did shortly thereafter recant his earlier full admission of guilt, claiming instead that he had acted alone and that his mother had no knowledge of the deed.

This would add an impediment to the state's case against the Meakers, as the prosecution could then not use the boy's new confession against Emeline. They were tried and housed separately at prison.

The dead girl's stomach was sent to a laboratory and strychnine tests were performed using a frog fed bits of the undigested elements found in the girl's stomach. The frog exhibited obvious signs of poison. Other tests were performed and the conclusive result was that the girl had been poisoned with strychnine.

A more sensational and disquieting event could hardly be conjured up from the bony soil of those hardscrabble hill farms of Vermont.

Both mother and son were found guilty and sentenced to death. Emeline Meaker proved to be a downright foul prisoner. She attacked guards, and screamed and howled at all hours in what appeared to be an attempt to prove she was insane. When that gambit grew old, she eventually settled into a begrudging prison routine.

In October 1882, four months before he was due to hang, Almon Meaker confessed in full, implicating his mother and detailing her role as mastermind of the entire affair. This led the court to repeal its decision of the death penalty for Almon, and instead they gave him life in prison.

Despite her son's pleas in a letter and in a face-to-face meeting trying to persuade her to admit her guilt—he told her it would "help ease your conscience"—Emeline refused.

On the day of her death, March 30, 1883, Emeline Meaker donned a new dress made for her by the women's warden, was given a large morning meal of a beefsteak, potatoes, bread and butter, meat pie, and coffee. Then she received visitors—among them Sheriff Atherton, to whom she again proclaimed her innocence and begged that he tell her husband and daughter she loved them. Later she asked to see the scaffold. The warden led her there and she said, "It's not as bad as I guessed it would be."

Following this, the hefty woman was given another meal, somewhat lighter than her first, and then led to the scaffold. Emeline was so deaf, that the final instructions and request of her for any final words had to be handed to her on slips of paper.

She read the note, and then said, "I am as innocent as that man right there," Emeline said, pointing at a nearby deputy. Officials shackled her hands and feet and slipped a black hood over her head. She could be heard muttering, "Oh, Christ! Oh, Christ!" And then the child-abusing murderess dropped. Her neck snapped like a carrot, she twitched and jounced, and she was pronounced dead several minutes later.

Horace bowed to pressure and did not grant his wife's wish of being buried in the family plot. Locals had objected, saying she had no right to be buried near the girl whose life she stole. Instead, Emeline Meaker was buried in the potter's field at Vermont State Prison in Windsor, Vermont.

And so we end the tragic Meaker tale with explanations for it all, save for the motive—and that's where it all goes muddy. One plausible motive put forth in news accounts of the time hinted that Almon and his mother, Emeline, may have been involved in an incestuous relationship, an episode of which could have been witnessed by poor Alice. To prevent the girl from telling others of this unlawful and forbidden association, Emeline could have convinced Almon that they had to kill the girl.

No matter the motive, the result is the same. What a dear mother.

An oversexed harpy? An ignorant, scheming bloodsucker? All of the above? In truth, a clear definition of the sort of person Mary Rogers had been hardly seems relevant or necessary any more. As with Emeline Meaker, Mary Rogers was a foul, premeditating double murderer and a multiple attempter. But she was only tried for a single killing—and then hung for it. She earned her place in the jerks hall of fame.

From the accounts that exist, it appears that Mary Mabel Rogers was an oversexed young creature who had probably never played with a full deck in her brief life. Her parents' union was not one sanctioned by marriage, making Mary a bastard whose mother was a teenager with distinct mental deficiencies. As a new baby, Mary was given up for adoption. The mother's apple didn't drop far from the crabbed tree, though, for at the age of fifteen in 1898, Mary ended up marrying Marcus Rogers.

From his choice of bride, Marcus might not have been the sharpest knife in the drawer either, but love, as they say, is a blind thing. In this case it was deaf and dumb as well. No matter her background, Mary couldn't have asked for a more doting or devoted husband. If only she had been capable of returning such heady emotion.

Alas, it seems all the girl wanted was a good time with other men. And this she sought extensively. She went so far as to leave her husband whenever she became disgruntled—a frequent state for her—for weeks at a time, seeking fun and the favors of men decidedly not her husband. With all this carrying on, by 1901 she gave birth to a baby girl, the paternity of which was suspect.

By the time the baby reached six months of age, Mary had had enough of playing mommy. One day she ran screaming to a neighbor's house, exclaiming that she had accidentally dropped her baby. The neighbor ran back with her to find the infant unconscious and dying of a fractured skull. Her husband's family members were unconvinced that it was an accident, and they doubted that the child was even Marcus's.

Despite this Marcus remained true to her. But their marriage was plagued not only by Mary's wantonness but also by dire poverty. They argued incessantly, and when Marcus had to relocate to New York to work as a laborer on his brother's farm, Mary refused to accompany him. She instead stayed at a rooming house in Bennington. The poor man visited her as often as he could, pleading with her to return with him so that they might once again live as husband and wife. She refused.

In between his visits, she took on a number of paramours, chief among them a young man named Morris Knapp, with whom she had sexual relations and whom she hoped to marry. How this was going to happen was a matter entirely for Mary to conjure. And she did work on a plan.

While various schemes fomented in this strange little hussy's brain, she also worked up regular sexual relations with her landlady's two sons, Levi Perham, the oldest at twenty-eight, and Leon, the younger at eighteen. One night, in the company of Levi and her friend Stella Bates, Mary asked Levi to help her kill her husband, Marcus. For Levi's part, she would pay him what she called "five hundred clean dollars," which she claimed would come from cashing in her husband's life insurance policy.

Intoxicated, Levi agreed to do the deed. But when he awoke the next day and recalled the previous evening's discussion, he backed out of the agreement. Curiously, he did not go to the police with this information but went instead to his mother, who called Mary's request nothing more than idle chatter.

Not so with Levi's younger brother, Leon. He was far more impressionable and eager to please this pretty young woman who fulfilled his sexual desires on a steady basis. When she asked him to help kill her husband, the youth agreed, despite the fact that he knew she fully intended to marry Morris Knapp afterward.

With an assistant in place, Mary Rogers then lured her husband to Bennington on the pretense of seeking reconciliation. They met early in the day on August 12, 1902. She suggested they meet again later, at 11 p.m. that evening, at Morgan's Grove, a treed spot alongside the Walloomsac River. Not surprisingly, the still-besotted Marcus agreed.

When he showed up, he found she'd been accompanied by Leon Perham. They all talked for a while, with poor unwitting Marcus relaxing into her sticky web. She held his head in her lap and spoke of her urge to reconcile. She smoothed his hair and smiled and talked glibly of their coming time together.

Soon enough, she sat up and told him that she had learned a rope trick earlier in the day, and she wanted to show it to Marcus. Little did he know she'd rehearsed what was about to happen.

First she tried the trick on Leon, tying his hands behind his back. He easily broke free several times. She claimed she must not have done it right, and she tried it on Marcus. He also broke free. Then she told Leon to try it on Marcus.

Once again, poor unwitting Marcus acquiesced to his estranged wife's wishes, thinking it all part of the fun. No doubt he was too excited at the prospect of winning back his gadfly wife's affections to heed any warnings of irregularity his senses should have offered.

Marcus soon found his hands bound for real, no trickery this time, while Mary rummaged in her purse for a bottle of chloroform. Leon struggled with the flailing husband, but he managed to subdue Marcus Rogers enough for Mary to keep the chloroform-soaked hankie jammed against his mouth and nose.

Despite being held down, Marcus was a tough man and flailed and bucked. It must have finally dawned on him that his little lovely wife had finally decided to end their troubled marriage, but not in a way that would have been beneficial to them both. Several times he lashed out with his legs, and Mary screamed to Leon, "Hold his legs! Hold his legs!"

It took twenty minutes for the chloroform to subdue the thrashing Marcus Rogers. And even then, he did not die but became hopelessly unconscious. Mary told Leon to cut the ropes free of Marcus's bound hands, and then she rummaged in her husband's pockets until she found his life insurance payment booklet.

Just what she'd need, she figured, for a life free of monetary woe. Though how much of a policy could the man have taken out? He was a dirt-poor laborer. Mary instructed the foolish youth to push her husband into the river.

As Marcus drifted downstream, Leon, once again per Mary's instructions, tacked Marcus's hat and a suicide note to the trunk of a riverbank tree. Mary had written the note earlier in the day, using her own nearly illiterate lingo and penmanship:

*Blame no one as I have at last put an end to my miseberl*
*life as my wife nows I have every threatened it, every nows*
*I have not anything or no body to live for no one can blame*
*me and so blame no one as my last request. Marcus Rogers*
*P. s. May i ope you will be happy*

Mary Rogers was thorough and brazen—if not overly intelligent. The next morning she headed straight to the sheriff's office and, crying, exclaimed that her dear husband was missing. She felt sure, she said between sniffles, that Marcus Rogers might well do himself harm, as they had argued just the day before.

She then visited two of Marcus's relatives, the sisters Phillipott, and repeated her story of woe and concern for poor Marcus, adding that she felt sure he may have drowned himself. What Mary did not realize was that Marcus had visited them only the night before. In fact, they were the only people other than his killers who could claim to have seen the hapless man alive that night.

They also knew that he had had his life insurance booklet with him, as he had shown it to them. He had also left his umbrella and some medicine with them and intended to retrieve the items the next day. So their suspicions were naturally aroused when Mary came along, brandishing the booklet before them and conjuring up crocodile tears on behalf of a husband they all knew she despised. Not a bright penny was Mary.

Oddly enough, it took a day before anyone noticed the dead man's hat pinned to the tree, then another day before anyone sought to investigate it further, discovering the note beneath. Two days after the murder, Marcus Rogers was found downstream, in two feet of water, face down near the bottom.

Marcus Rogers's body was autopsied, and during the procedure, Mary Rogers insisted on being right there while they cut open her husband. During the proceedings she evinced no sign of consternation at seeing her dead husband's body laid out, cut into, poked, and prodded. On the contrary, she inquired several times whether there was any sign of poison. To the doctors and others in attendance, she seemed smug in her questioning, as if daring them to find anything amiss with his death.

Marcus's body was brought to Mary's boardinghouse and laid out on a table directly beneath her room on the second floor. That same night she tried twice, the second time via a messenger, to summon Knapp, her lover, to her room. He refused, saying in a return note that she ought to be better behaved, considering her dead husband was laid out in the room beneath.

If people suspected Mary Rogers of oddness before her husband's death, they fast became convinced that the foul, lying creature was like no one the community had ever seen before. Days later, at the coroner's inquest, Mary instructed Leon Perham and his mother to say that her husband's death had been a suicide. But at the inquest, the coroner's reports all pointed toward foul play, as the dead man had no water in his lungs, and thus he could not have drowned. He also had a large bruise on his temple, possible evidence of having been subdued somehow. Further evidence of foul play soon stacked up.

Mary was kept outside the courtroom, sequestered during part of the proceedings. And then Levi Perham was called to the stand, where he explained how Mary had previously approached him and asked him to do away with her husband for money. Young Leon Perham, visibly shaken, was also called to the stand. And he cracked like a thin-shelled egg, confessing the crime and explained the entire chain of events leading to it.

Mary was then called in. Unaware of all that had transpired during the inquest, she rambled on about how much she loved her husband. She also made up stories about her whereabouts on the day of his death. Her obvious outright fabrications were soon disproven and she was arrested, feigning innocence the entire time.

Because he confessed to the crime unbidden and seemed genuinely remorseful, Leon Perham was not sentenced to hang. But Mary Rogers's long trial would not be so kind to her. Her defense attorneys could do little to help make her appear as they would have wished. Prosecutors trotted out a number of people who had known her for a long time, and the cumulative effects of their testimonies added up to a sad result: Mary Rogers was a shameless harlot who had been repeatedly adulterous.

In February 1905 she was found guilty of murder and sentenced to hang. The sentence, thought not undeserved, came as a shock to many, as only one woman had been put to death in Vermont—Emeline Meaker on March 30, 1883—though it was agreed that they were both premeditated murderesses.

A bill was introduced to the Vermont House of Representatives to commute Rogers's sentence to life imprisonment. There was strong support of this, despite the fact—or perhaps because of it—that the man who introduced the bill, Frank C. Archibald, a Vermont state representative himself, was also one of her defense attorneys.

It was determined that Mary Rogers's mental health should be assessed, both before and after the crime. If she was found to be unstable in either instance, she might well be reprieved of the death penalty. The issue went all the way to the US Supreme Court, which found, on November 27, 1905, that her rights were not violated by the state of Vermont's judicial system, which meant that the original sentence was upheld.

It later came out that Mary had been pregnant at the time of her husband's murder. She had suspected her condition before the murder, and, as she did not want to be pregnant, she had visited a doctor who confirmed her suspicions. She then threatened the doctor's life because he refused to give her powerful drugs that would terminate the pregnancy.

In the interim, Mary Rogers had been a busy girl at the Vermont State Prison in Windsor. Apparently, she had been having numerous sexual liaisons with a prison trusty—a convicted rapist who had access to the locks on the doors of her outer cell. Mary herself had used a pair of scissors (she'd been crocheting aprons as gifts for many of her supporters) to pick the locks on the inside of her cell.

When the rapist and the killer met, they coupled a number of times over the course of ten days. This was revealed in an investigation, and it was suspected that she had been trying to become pregnant in hopes of preventing her execution—or at least prolonging the inevitable.

But that never happened. And the scaffold was dusted off, a solid-oak affair stored in the prison attic and not used since 1891.

The numbered pieces were assembled, and new rope was rigged in accordance with the law, weight, and tradition.

On December 8, 1905, without having eaten breakfast— apparently her predicament might have begun to nibble at her rough edges—Mary Rogers was hung by the neck until dead at the Vermont State Prison. Unfortunately for her, the rope stretched, her feet hit the floor, and guards were forced to lift the rope for the entire fourteen minutes it took for Mary Rogers to die a slow, painful death.

These two dreadfuls didn't know each other, but they shared a number of common traits such as greed and selfishness that would make a professional gambler blush, and an utter disregard of others. They also share footnote space in the pages of Vermont's history: Meaker was the first woman legally executed in Vermont, and Mary Rogers was the last woman to hold that distinction. And they were the last two women legally executed in New England.

## CHAPTER 20

# Dr. Henry F. Perkins:
## *Eugenicist, Purveyor of Purity*

From the late 1800s into the early 1900s, followers of the pseudoscience known as eugenics (the promotion of racial purity through science) proselytized throughout the United States about the wonders of their cause as much as devotees of any religion. Soon, widespread support of the American eugenics movement ushered in a frightening period of mass hysteria and brainwashing based on the crusade's pseudoscientific beliefs and findings.

One of eugenics' biggest proponents, University of Vermont zoology professor Dr. Henry Farnham Perkins, spearheaded witch hunts in his own state that resulted in the sterilization (and worse) of entire groups of everyday Vermonters whom the eugenicists considered "deficients." Perkins was not exactly the warm-and-fuzzy type.

Sir Francis Galton coined the term *eugenics* in 1883 and defined it as "the study of all agencies under human control which can improve or impair the racial quality of future generations." Eugenics has also been called an attempt to promote racial purity through science and a way to improve human genetic qualities. It was considered a method of preventative medical care in an effort to ward off undesirable physical and mental health effects—something most of us are guilty of pursuing, however dismally, every time we hop on a treadmill or try to quit smoking.

The eugenics movement that Galton's early work spawned soon mutated into an aberrant outgrowth fueled increasingly by the personal biases of a small number of elitists who had a tendency to look upon their fellows as inferiors and frequently as deficients.

All those definitions, however, can't disguise the fact that eugenics was an insidious, pseudoscientific excuse for widespread forced sterilization, incarceration, institutionalization, racial segregation,

In the first part of the twentieth century in America, misguided followers of the pseudoscience eugenics believed they could promote racial purity through science. They also directly influenced Adolf Hitler's quest for racial supremacy.

and segregation of the mentally and physically ill. Its practitioners used it as an excuse to advocate euthanasia and even genocide of individuals, families, and entire races of people who were considered by a handful of self-appointed elites as inferior and unworthy of being allowed to coexist with the rest of society.

In theory, eugenics sounds logical, even useful. But as with so many such concepts, once it was put into practice, it was found to be a miserable, damaging failure, generating a frightening period of mass hysteria, brainwashing, and witch hunts that raged in the United States for decades. In its repurposed form, the movement leeched beyond US shores, spreading influence worldwide to such places as Nazi Germany, where, inspired by the American eugenics movement, Adolf Hitler began experimenting on his own people. As we all know, his reprehensible attempts at racial purification resulted in the deaths of millions of innocent people.

Despite such horrific and unfortunate results, eugenics still had ardent proponents hawking its dubious wares long past the movement's sell-by date. Even decades later, once the misdeeds and misery they caused were exposed and eugenicists found themselves at the bottom of their long, slippery slope, few in the movement gave much thought to the human wreckage they left behind.

Vermont's own poster boy for genetic purity, Henry F. Perkins, was born in Burlington, Vermont, on May 10, 1877, into a large, well-to-do family with a long lineage tracing back to *Mayflower* passengers. Perkins came by his academic interests through exposure to his educator-father's pursuits. Perkins the elder was a noted naturalist and professor of geology at the University of Vermont (UVM) in Burlington. Henry Perkins graduated from UVM in 1898 and then went on to earn his doctorate in zoology at Johns Hopkins in 1902. He returned to UVM to teach and stayed there until his retirement in 1945.

In the years following World War I, Dr. Perkins grew alarmed at the results of a study showing higher-than-national-average incidences of so-called defects in men from Vermont who had joined the Army during the war. The findings described high rates of diabetes and epilepsy, as well as other so-called deficiencies and deformities.

Dr. Perkins, who considered himself an old-line Vermonter, sought to broaden his new UVM course offering on heredity and evolution. Already a student of and heavily influenced by the growing national eugenics movement, Perkins felt that his own research might help address the causes of the troubling survey results and instigate solutions to help reduce deficiencies and cull undesirable genetic traits, resulting in a pure, strong strain of Vermonter.

He went about this in a systematic, orderly manner, beginning in 1925 with his Eugenics Survey, the purpose of which he stated was "to gather information, as full and accurate as possible, that can be used for social betterment in Vermont—that is, for the ultimate improvement in the quality of our citizens."

As an old-stock Yankee from a long-established line, Perkins wanted to remove from the world any people that would be considered of lower class, those people whose family histories and genetic traits marked them, in the eyes of eugenicists, as useless. Perkins took it upon himself to set up the studies based on research and public education, and to drum up support for legislation to reduce what he called Vermont's "social problem group."

So convinced was Dr. Perkins of the need for a genetic hoeing out of what he perceived as the weeds in Vermont's "seedbed" that he wanted to "make the waste places of the state bloom like the rose." Had his methods of achieving these admirable ideals not callously disregarded the lives of the families Perkins and his fellow eugenicists considered "dependent, delinquent, and deficient," he might have been able to provide something of genuine worth to science instead of marginalizing thousands of Vermonters and nearly wiping out the native Abenaki people.

While eugenics and the pursuit of it existed in Vermont before Perkins's survey, the Eugenics Survey of Vermont did become the state's official mouthpiece for the national eugenics movement. Emboldened and buoyed by national interest in the movement, Perkins's supporters cast their net wider. So fervently did they believe in the study and promotion of eugenics that they sought to inculcate "a eugenic consciousness" in the state. They planned to exert control of what they called the "underclass" by strict social planning, education, and perhaps most frightening of all, reproductive control.

They went about this methodically, knocking on doors, turning a keen ear to small-town gossip, and leaving no potential deficient unmolested. And what they found they measured against their own genetic yardstick, frequently finding their subjects wanting.

Perkins's study sought out what it deemed evidence to help make his case, in the form of social records from towns, officials from towns, and anecdotal evidence from what they called "informants," frequently neighbors with a grudge. They labeled their findings "bad heredity" in more than sixty Vermont families.

This evidence was used as the basis for drumming up support for instigation of hopefully reversing such "bad heredity" by implementing sexual sterilization, expanding institutions for the feeble minded, and mental testing of anyone deemed at risk of being a carrier of bad heredity who also used public institutions such as public schools or public family welfare, and of all people within the criminal justice system. Armed with this dubious scientific information, and with the self-righteous attitude of one who sees himself as a paragon of virtue, Perkins spoke before the Vermont state legislature to help further his pet project, a campaign for a statewide sterilization law.

Within the survey, the section titled "Pedigrees of Degenerate Families" was so far removed from scientific basis that it smacked of outright prejudice. Even Perkins himself, in 1928, put a halt to this aspect of the study, claiming it was "not sufficiently scientific."

But it was too little, too late. Families throughout Vermont who had been labeled by Perkins's survey as "degenerates" were now publicly painted as not much better than lowly animals worthy of being destroyed. They were pointed out as social menaces, burdens on the taxpaying public, and worse. People who had formerly been friendly to them now rejected them, they were under intense social and governmental scrutiny, and numerous family members were institutionalized and sterilized.

Based on the strength of what was perceived publicly as a successful study, in 1927 Perkins was able to procure funding sufficient enough to begin what he called the Vermont Commission on Country Life (VCCL), an intense scrutiny of rural people and communities throughout Vermont that lasted from 1928 to 1931. During that time, Perkins was careful to avoid potential public confusion with his previous survey, lest the public become skittish that they might well end up sterilized! He suspended the sterilization campaign during this time, and the VCCL now labeled his former targets—previously known by him as those with "bad heredity"—as "the handicapped."

The VCCL sought to build up the notion of what it called "good old Vermont stock" and promote the strong genetic traits found in old Vermont families by stating the following:

> It is clear that if the valuable characteristics of our old Vermont stock are to be conserved and passed on to future generations for the good of the state and the nation, conditions must be brought about which will favor the maintenance of that stock as far as possible. . . To promote the best future citizenry in the state, this Commission makes the following recommendations:
>
> 1. That Vermonters be encouraged to keep and study their own family records with a view to arousing their pride in the achievements and high qualities of their ancestral stock so that this pride may in turn stimulate their better efforts and guide them in their choice of mates.
> 2. That the doctrine be spread that it is the patriotic duty of every normal couple to have children in sufficient number to keep up to par the "good old Vermont stock."
>
> —VCCL, Rural Vermont: A Program for the Future, "The People"

DR. HENRY F. PERKINS

The VCCL drew a strong and definite distinction between its valued "good old Vermont stock" and those "handicapped" Vermonters it had already targeted and separated out of the herd socially. This methodical approach led to expanded state programs that prevented marriage and reproduction in those individuals it deemed "feeble minded," which included many non-English-speaking Vermont residents such as Abenaki Indians and French Canadians, people who were just as intelligent as their fellow Vermonters but were unable to defend themselves in English when run aground by Perkins and his cohorts. The VCCL claimed, in part, that such individuals were unfit to breed and raise offspring.

The most infamous of reforms resulting from Perkins's strident efforts became his crowning achievement: the 1931 Vermont Sterilization Law: "A Law for Human Betterment by Voluntary Sterilization." This made Vermont the twenty-fourth state to adopt a compulsory sterilization law. Nationally, thirty-three states would do the same, resulting in the sterilization of sixty-five thousand people nationwide between the years 1907 and 1981.

In 1927, US Supreme Court associate justice Oliver Wendell Holmes Jr. was so swayed by the propaganda of the burgeoning eugenics movement that he wrote, "It is better for all the world, if instead of waiting to execute degenerate offspring for crime, or to let them starve for their imbecility, society can prevent those who are manifestly unfit from continuing their kind. The principle that sustains compulsory vaccination is broad enough to cover cutting the Fallopian tubes."

In the Green Mountain State, Perkins's astounding piece of legislation targeted specific groups, most notably French Canadians and native Vermonters such as the Abenaki Indians, descendants of people who inhabited the region far earlier than Perkins's allegedly superior Yankee stock.

If the rural poor in Vermont suffered mightily at the hands of Dr. Perkins and his Eugenics Survey, the Abenaki Indians were the hardest hit of all targeted racial groups. Many Abenaki moved from their home state, changed their names, or adopted low-profile lives in an effort to escape Perkins's ever-encroaching witch hunt. Many Abenaki did their best to blend in with the French-Canadian population, but even in this group they were vilified, as French Canadians were deemed by the Eugenics Survey to also be deficients. Numerous Abenaki, tracked down by Perkins's "social workers," were forced into institutions and unwillingly sterilized.

Official records claim two hundred to three hundred such cases of sterilization in Vermont, a modest figure by national eugenics standards of the time, but anecdotal evidence suggests the figure was significantly higher—perhaps in the thousands.

In a number of instances, Abenaki, French-speaking women, and men and women who were unable for a variety of reasons to comprehend or respond to questions put to them in medical exams were deemed to have agreed to sterilization. Many more were simply sterilized without their consent, and a number of women of the so-called group of deficients who went to doctors for prenatal medical exams mysteriously lost their unborn babies soon thereafter.

It is this state-sanctioned sterilization that is undoubtedly Perkins's lasting legacy, but it is by no means the only scar he helped inflict on the social landscape of the Green Mountain State.

Unsatisfied with his "progress," in 1931 Perkins began serving as president of the American Eugenics Society, banging his VCCL gong nationwide as an ideal model eugenics program for the United States.

Though the Eugenics Survey came to a close in 1936, UVM continued to teach eugenics, as did other institutions of higher learning and high schools throughout Vermont, for decades to come. The state's Department of Public Welfare and other agencies continued to identify, register, sterilize, and intervene in families with children deemed "backward," all in the hopes of preventing unwanted, unfit Vermonters from popping up and tainting Perkins's "good old Vermont stock."

The instigation of state-sanctioned sterilization, institutionalization, and killing is not a legacy of which to be proud. Dr. Henry Perkins and a number of other well-intentioned but deluded individuals will be most remembered for their part in these witch hunts based on the pseudoscience that inspired Adolf Hitler's mass genocide campaigns. But some of the seeds of his mad pursuits had been planted in the United States decades before.

As early as 1911, a report from the Carnegie Institute recommended euthanasia, or the "painless killing of a patient suffering from an incurable or painful disease, or in an irreversible coma," as a "solution" to help cleanse society of genetic tendencies and attributes a self-appointed elite few deemed as unacceptable. The Carnegie report advocated establishing regional gas chambers throughout the United States in which to exterminate the deficients.

Despite the overall agreement on this course of action among the movers and shakers in the eugenics movement, it was also acknowledged that such widespread, large-scale mercy killing might make average Americans a little queasy. Instead, alternative forms of euthanasia were suggested, chief among them was allowing doctors to perform the final deed on their own, case by case, as they saw fit.

Incoming patients at a mental institution in Lincoln, Illinois, for example, were fed tuberculosis-tainted milk on the assumption that if the individual were genetically fit, he or she would survive. Unfortunately that stunning logic didn't follow through—death rates ranged from 30 to 40 percent. In the same state, in 1931, the Homeopathic Medicine Association sought the right to kill "imbeciles." And 1938 saw the founding of the Euthanasia Society of America.

Eugenics in New England wasn't relegated solely to the green hills of Vermont. In 1908 in Exeter, Rhode Island, Dr. Joseph H. Ladd established the Rhode Island School for the Feeble-Minded (later called the Ladd School), modeled on the Templeton Colony at the Massachusetts School for the Feeble-Minded, where he had previously worked, and where he had trained under famed eugenicist Dr. Walter Fernald. Within a few years of its opening, the already overcrowded Rhode Island facility became a convenient place for the state to dump people deemed unworthy, for widely varying reasons, to live in "civilized" society. These included young women who became pregnant out of wedlock, petty thieves, and rapists.

The faulty facility limped along, soaked in scandal—unexplained deaths, rapes, murder, abuse—until 1993, when it was finally closed.

In 1912, on the authority of Maine governor Frederick W. Plaisted, the mixed-race residents of Malaga Island, a forty-one-acre island in the New Meadows River in Maine's Casco Bay, were forcibly evicted from their longtime homes. Many of them were relocated to the Maine School for the Feeble-Minded, others were left homeless, unwanted by local towns. Even the residents of the island's cemetery were exhumed and the bodies relocated, buried unceremoniously and without markers, in the graveyard at the same state facility.

# Bibliography

Abbott, Geoffrey. *The Executioner Always Chops Twice: Ghastly Blunders on the Scaffold.* New York: St. Martin's Press, 2002.

Acheson, James M. *The Lobster Gangs of Maine.* Lebanon, NH: University Press of New England, 1988.

Adams, Brewster. *The Prospector: Values in the Rough.* Reno, NV: Reno Printing, 1940.

Balkan, Evan. *Shipwrecked! Deadly Adventures and Disasters at Sea.* Birmingham, AL: Menasha Ridge, 2008.

Beckius, Kim Knox. *Backroads of New England: Your Guide to New England's Most Scenic Backroad Adventures.* St. Paul, MN: Voyageur Press/MBI Publishing, 2004.

Belanger, Jeff, ed. *Encyclopedia of Haunted Places: Ghostly Locales from Around the World.* Edison, NJ: Castle Books, 2008.

Bell, Michael E. *Food for the Dead: On the Trail of New England's Vampires.* New York: Carroll & Graf, 2001.

Bellamy, John Stark, II. *Vintage Vermont Villainies: True Tales of Murder and Mystery from the 19th and 20th Centuries.* Woodstock, VT: Countryman Press, 2007.

Bellesiles, Michael A. *Revolutionary Outlaws: Ethan Allen and the Struggle for Independence on the Early American Frontier.* Charlottesville: University Press of Virginia, 1993.

Binder, Jeff. New Hampshire. *Compass American Guides.* New York: Fodor's, 2002.

Blanton, DeAnne, and Lauren M. Cook. *They Fought Like Demons: Women Soldiers in the American Civil War.* Baton Rouge: Louisiana State University Press, 2002.

Block, Lawrence, ed. *Gangsters, Swindlers, Killers & Thieves: The Lives & Crimes of Fifty American Villains.* New York: Oxford University Press, 2004.

Bondeson, Jan. *The Great Pretenders: The True Stories Behind Famous Historical Mysteries.* New York: W. W. Norton, 2004.

Boylan, Brian Richard. *Benedict Arnold: The Dark Eagle.* New York: W. W. Norton, 1973.

Bross, Tom, Patricia Harris, and David Lyon, contributors. *DK Eyewitness Travel Guide: Boston.* New York: Dorling Kindersley, 2001.

Bruinius, Harry. *Better for All the World: The Secret History of Forced Sterilization and America's Quest for Racial Purity.* New York: Alfred A. Knopf, 2006.

Bryson, Bill. *The Lost Continent: Travels in Small-Town America.* New York: Harper Perennial, 1990.

Buker, George E. *The Penobscot Expedition: Commodore Saltonstall and the Massachusetts Conspiracy of 1779.* Annapolis, MD: Naval Institute Press, 2002.

Caldwell, Bill. *Rivers of Fortune: Where Maine Tides and Money Flowed.* Portland, ME: Guy Gannett, 1983.

Campbell, Susan, and Bruce Gellerman. *The Big Book of New England Curiosities: From Orange, CT, to Blue Hill, ME, a Guide to the Quirkiest, Oddest, and Most Unbelievable Stuff You'll See.* Guilford, CT: Globe Pequot Press, 2009.

Chenoweth, James. *Oddity Odyssey: A Journey through New England's Colorful Past.* New York: Henry Holt, 1996.

Citro, Joseph A. *Green Mountains, Dark Tales.* Lebanon, NH: University Press of New England, 2001.

———. *Passing Strange: True Tales of New England Hauntings and Horrors.* Shelburne, VT: Chapters Publishing, 1996.

Clifford, Barry. *Expedition Whydah: The Story of the World's First Excavation of a Pirate Treasure Ship and the Man Who Found Her.* New York: HarperCollins, 1999.

Cole, John N. *Maine Trivia.* Nashville, TN: Rutledge Hill Press, 1998.

Cordingly, David. *Women Sailors and Sailors' Women.* New York: Random House, 2001.

Cottle, Samuel S. *In Danger at Sea: Adventures of a New England Fishing Family.* Camden, ME: Down East Books, 2007.

Cronon, William. *Changes in the Land: Indians, Colonists and the Ecology of New England.* New York: Hill and Wang/Farrar-Straus & Giroux, 1983.

Druett, John. *She Captains: Heroines and Hellions of the Sea.* New York: Simon & Schuster, 2000.

Eckstorm, Fannie Hardy. *Penobscot Man.* Bangor, ME: Fannie Hardy Eckstorm, 1931.

Feintuch, Burt, and David H. Watters, eds. *The Encyclopedia of New England.* New Haven, CT: Yale University Press, 2005.

Felton, Bruce, and Mark Fowler. *Felton & Fowler's Famous Americans You Never Knew Existed.* New York: Stein and Day, 1979.

Fish, Charles. *In Good Hands: The Keeping of a Family Farm.* New York: Kodansha Globe, 1996.

Fleming, Thomas. *Liberty! The American Revolution.* New York: Viking/Penguin, 1997.

Fowler, William W. *Frontier Women.* Stamford, CT: Longmeadow Press, 1995.

Freedman, Lew. *The Way We Were New England: Nostalgic Images of America's Northeast.* Guilford, CT: Globe Pequot Press, 2009.

Friedlander, Henri. *The Origins of Nazi Genocide*. Chapel Hill: University of North Carolina Press, 1997.

Gallagher, Nancy. *Breeding Better Vermonters*. Lebanon, NH: University Press of New England, 1999.

Garland, Joseph E. *Eastern Point: A Nautical, Rustical, and Social Chronicle of Gloucester's Outer Shield and Inner Sanctum, 1606–1950*. Peterborough, NH: Noone House, 1971.

Goldberg, M. Hirsh. *The Blunder Book*. New York: William Morrow, 1984.

Greenlaw, Linda. *The Lobster Chronicles: Life on a Very Small Island*. New York: Hyperion, 2002.

Hall, Richard. *Patriots in Disguise: Women Warriors of the Civil War*. New York: Paragon House, 1993.

Hansen, Harry, ed. *New England Legends and Folklore*. New York: Hastings House, 1967.

Harper's Magazine. *New England: A Collection from Harper's Magazine*. New York: Gallery Books, 1990.

Hauck, Dennis William. *Haunted Places: The National Directory*. New York: Penguin, 2002.

Higginson, Thomas Wentworth. *Travelers and Outlaws: Episodes in American History*. New York: Lee and Shepard, 1889.

Hill, Ralph Nading. *Yankee Kingdom: Vermont and New Hampshire*. New York: Harper, 1960.

Holland, Barbara. *Brief Histories & Heroes*. Pleasantville, NY: Akadine Press, 1998.

Johnson, Claudia Durst. *Daily Life in Colonial New England*. Westport, CT: Greenwood Press, 2002.

Johnson, Dorothy M., and R. T. Turner. *The Bedside Book of Bastards: A Rich Collection of Counterirritants to the Exasperations of Contemporary Life.* New York: Barnes & Noble Books, 1994.

Jones, Eric. *New Hampshire Curiosities: Quirky Characters, Roadside Oddities & Other Offbeat Stuff.* Guilford, CT: Globe Pequot Press, 2006.

Jordan, Charles J. *Tales Told in the Shadows of the White Mountains.* Lebanon, NH: University Press of New England, 2003.

Lemke, William. *The Wild, Wild East: Unusual Tales of Maine History.* Camden, ME: Yankee Books, 1990.

Lepore, Jill. *The Name of War: King Philip's War and the Origins of American Identity.* New York: Alfred A. Knopf, 1998.

Lippincott, Bertram. *Indians, Privateers, and High Society: A Rhode Island Sampler.* New York: J. B. Lippincott, 1961.

Mayo, Matthew P. *Bootleggers, Lobstermen, and Lumberjacks: Fifty of the Grittiest Moments in the History of Hardscrabble New England.* Guilford, CT: Globe Pequot Press, 2011.

McCain, Diana Ross. *Mysteries and Legends of New England: True Stories of the Unsolved and Unexplained.* Guilford, CT: Globe Pequot Press, 2009.

McDevitt, Neale, ed. *Eyewitness Travel Guides New England.* New York: Dorling Kindersley, 2001.

Mitchell, Don. *Compass American Guides: Vermont.* New York: Fodor's, 1999.

Morgan, Edmund S. *American Heroes: Profiles of Men and Women Who Shaped Early America.* New York: W. W. Norton, 2009.

Morison, Samuel Eliot. *The Maritime History of Massachusetts 1783–1860.* Boston: Northeastern University Press, 1979.

Murphy, Jim. *The Real Benedict Arnold.* New York: Clarion Books, 2007.

Murray, Stuart. *Eyewitness Books: American Revolution.* New York: Dorling Kindersley, 2002.

Muse, Vance. *Smithsonian Guide to Historic America: Northern New England.* New York: Stewart, Tabori & Chang, 1989.

Oppel, Frank, ed. *Tales of the New England Coast.* Secaucus, NJ: Castle Books, 1985.

Pettengill, Samuel B. *The Yankee Pioneers: A Saga of Courage.* Rutland, VT: Charles E. Tuttle, 1971.

Philbrick, Nathaniel. *Mayflower: A Story of Courage, Community, and War.* New York: Penguin, 2007.

Philbrook, Kate, and Rob Rosenthal. *Malaga Island: A Story Best Left Untold.* Photo/radio documentary from WMPG-FM and Salt Institute for Documentary Studies, 2008, malagaislandmaine.org/.

Philips, David E. *Legendary Connecticut: Traditional Tales from the Nutmeg State.* Willimantic, CT: Curbstone Press, 1992.

Pike, Robert, E. *Spiked Boots.* Dublin, NH: Yankee Books, 1987.

———. *Tall Trees, Trough Men.* New York: W. W. Norton, 1999.

Platt, Camille Smith. *Real Cheesy Facts About: Famous Authors.* Birmingham, AL: Crane Hill Publishers, 2006.

Quinn, William P. *Shipwrecks around New England: A Chronology of Marine Accidents and Disasters from Grand Manan to Sandy Hook.* Orleans, MA: Lower Cape Publishing, 1979.

Rapaport, Diane. *The Naked Quaker: True Crimes and Controversies from the Courts of Colonial New England.* Beverly, MA: Commonwealth Editions, 2007.

Rogak, Lisa. *Stones and Bones of New England: A Guide to Unusual, Historic, and Otherwise Notable Cemeteries.* Guilford, CT: Globe Pequot Press, 2004.

Rolde, Neil/WCBB. *So You Think You Know Maine.* Gardiner, ME: Harpswell Press, 1984.

Rondina, Christopher. *Vampires of New England.* Dennis, MA: On Cape Publications, 2008.

Russell, Howard S. *A Long, Deep Furrow: Three Centuries of Farming in New England.* Hanover, NH: University Press of New England, 1982.

Schechter, Harold. *Fatal: The Poisonous Life of a Female Serial Killer.* New York: Simon & Schuster, 2003.

Schlosser, S. E. *Spooky New England: Tales of Hauntings, Strange Happenings, and Other Local Lore.* Guilford, CT: Globe Pequot Press, 2003.

Seavey, Wendell. *Working the Sea: Misadventures, Ghost Stories, and Life Lessons from a Maine Lobsterfisherman.* Berkeley, CA: North Atlantic Books, 2005.

Sheinkin, Steve. *The Notorious Benedict Arnold: A True Story of Adventure, Heroism & Treachery.* New York: Roaring Brook Press, 2010.

Sherr, Lynn, and Jurate Kazickas. *Susan B. Anthony Slept Here: A Guide to American Women's Landmarks.* New York: Times Books/Random House, 1994.

Simons, D. Brenton. *Witches, Rakes, and Rogues: True Stories of Scam, Scandal, Murder, and Mayhem in Boston, 1630–1775.* Beverly, MA: Commonwealth Editions, 2005.

Sloane, Eric. *Diary of an Early American Boy: Noah Blake, 1805.* New York: Ballantine Books, 1965.

Smith, Joshua M. *Borderland Smuggling: Patriots, Loyalists, and Illicit Trade in the Northeast, 1783–1820.* Gainesville: University Press of Florida, 2006.

Snow, Edward Rowe. *Ghosts, Gales and Gold.* New York: Dodd, Mead, 1972.

———. *Tales of Terror and Tragedy.* New York: Dodd, Mead, 1980.

Stanley, Jo, ed. *Bold in Her Breeches: Women Pirates Across the Ages.* New York: HarperCollins, 1995.

St. Antoine, Sara, ed. *Stories from Where We Live: The North Atlantic Coast.* Minneapolis, MN: Milkweed Editions, 2000.

Starbuck, David R., ed. *Historical New Hampshire.* 49, no. 4 (Winter 1994). Concord: New Hampshire Historical Society, 1994.

Stephens, John Richard, ed. *Captured by Pirates: 22 Firsthand Accounts of Murder and Mayhem on the High Seas.* New York: Barnes & Noble Books, 2006.

Stevens, Peter F. *Notorious & Notable New Englanders.* Camden, ME: Down East Books, 1997.

Teller, Walter M., ed. *Twelve Works of Naïve Genius.* New York: Harcourt Brace Jovanovich, 1972.

Thornton, Brian. *The Book of Bastards: 101 Worst Scoundrels and Scandals from the World of Politics and Power.* Avon, MA: Adams Media, 2010.

Titler, Dale M. *Unnatural Resources: True Stories of American Treasure.* Englewood Cliffs, NJ: Prentice-Hall, 1973.

Tougias, Michael J. *Fatal Forecast: An Incredible True Tale of Disaster and Survival at Sea.* New York: Scribner, 2007.

Vaughan, Alden T. *New England Encounters: Indians and Euroamericans, ca. 1600–1850.* Lebanon, NH: University Press of New England, 1999.

————. *New England Frontier: Puritans and Indians 1620–1675.* Norman: University of Oklahoma Press, 1995.

Vietze, Andrew. *Insider's Guide to the Maine Coast.* 2nd ed. Guilford, CT: Globe Pequot Press, 2007.

Weir, William. *Written with Lead: America's Most Famous and Notorious Gunfights from the Revolutionary War to Today.* New York: Cooper Square Press, 2003.

Wheeler, Scott. *Rumrunners & Revenuers.* Shelburne, VT: New England Press, 2002.

Wiencek, Henry. *The Smithsonian Guide to Historic America: Southern New England.* New York: Stewart, Tabori & Chang, 1989.

Wilbur, C. Keith. *New England Indians: An Informed and Fascinating Account of the 18 Major Tribes that Lived in Pre-Colonial New England.* 2nd ed. Guilford, CT: Globe Pequot Press, 1996.

Woodard, Colin. *The Lobster Coast: Rebels, Rusticators, and the Struggle for a Forgotten Frontier.* New York: Viking/Penguin, 2004.

————. *The Republic of Pirates: Being the True and Surprising Story of the Caribbean Pirates and the Man Who Brought Them Down.* New York: Harcourt, 2007.

Young, Alfred F. *Masquerade: The Life and Times of Deborah Sampson, Continental Soldier.* New York: Alfred A. Knopf, 2004.

Zinn, Howard. *A People's History of the United States.* New York: HarperCollins, 2003.

# Index

# About the Author

**Matthew P. Mayo** is an award-winning author of more than twenty-five books and dozens of short stories. His novel, *Tucker's Reckoning*, won the Western Writers of America's 2013 Spur Award for Best Western Novel. He has also been a Spur Finalist in the Short Fiction category and a Western Fictioneers Peacemaker Award Finalist. His novels include *Winters' War*; *Wrong Town*; *Hot Lead, Cold Heart*; *Dead Man's Ranch*; *Tucker's Reckoning*; *The Hunted*, and more. He also contributes to other popular series of Western and adventure novels.

Matthew's non-fiction books include *Cowboys, Mountain Men & Grizzly Bears*; *Bootleggers, Lobstermen & Lumberjacks*; *Sourdoughs, Claim Jumpers & Dry Gulchers*; *Haunted Old West*; *Myths & Mysteries of New Hampshire*; *Jerks in New England History* (all Globe Pequot Press), and numerous others. He has collaborated with his wife, photographer Jennifer Smith-Mayo, on a series of hardcover books: *Maine Icons*, *New Hampshire Icons*, and *Vermont Icons* (all Globe Pequot Press).

The Mayos run Gritty Press (GrittyPress.com) and rove the world in search of hot coffee, tasty whiskey, and high adventure. Stop by Matthew's website for a chin-wag and a cup of mud at matthewmayo.com.